SARATOGA LOST

IMAGES OF VICTORIAN AMERICA

by

Robert Joki

BLACK · DOME

Black Dome Press Corp.
RR 1, Box 422
Hensonville, New York 12439

Published by
Black Dome Press Corp.
RR1, Box 422
Hensonville, New York 12439
Tel: (518) 734-6357
Fax: (518) 734-5802

Library of Congress Cataloging-in-Publication Data
Joki, Robert.
        Saratoga Lost: images of Victorian America/by Robert Joki.
            p. cm.
        Includes bibliographical references and index.
        ISBN 1-883789-15-X (trade pbk.)
        1. Saratoga Springs (N.Y.)—History—Pictorial works. 2. Historic buildings—New York
(State)—Saratoga Springs—Pictorial works. 3. Saratoga Springs (N.Y.)—Buildings,
structures, etc. —Pictorial works. I. Title.
F129.S3J65   1998
974.7'48—DC21   98—13208
                                                                                                     CIP

Design by Carol Clement, Artemisia, Inc.
Printed in the USA

For
Susan, Sara and Todd

TABLE OF CONTENTS

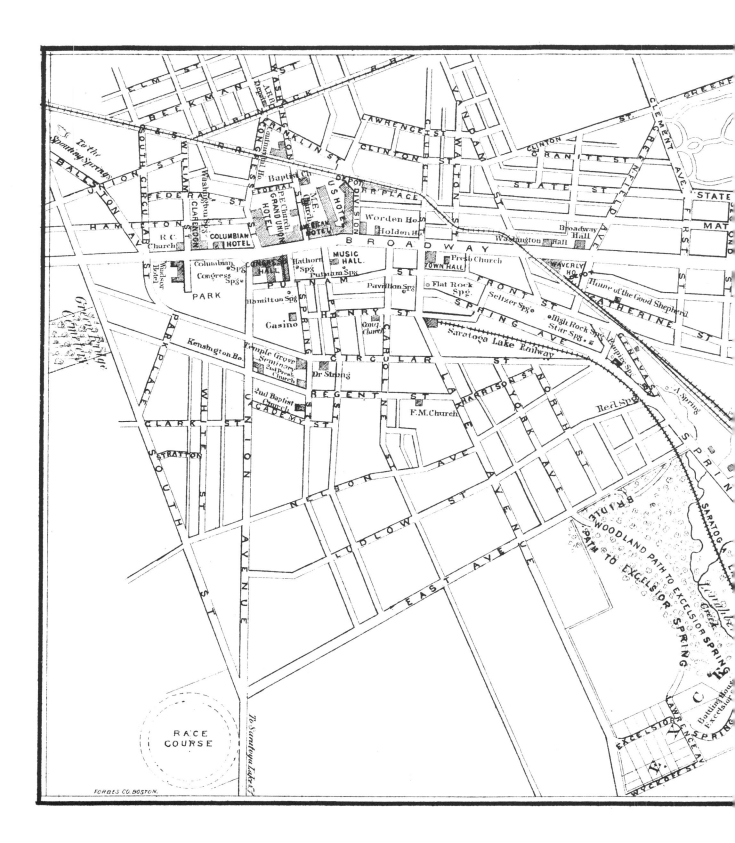

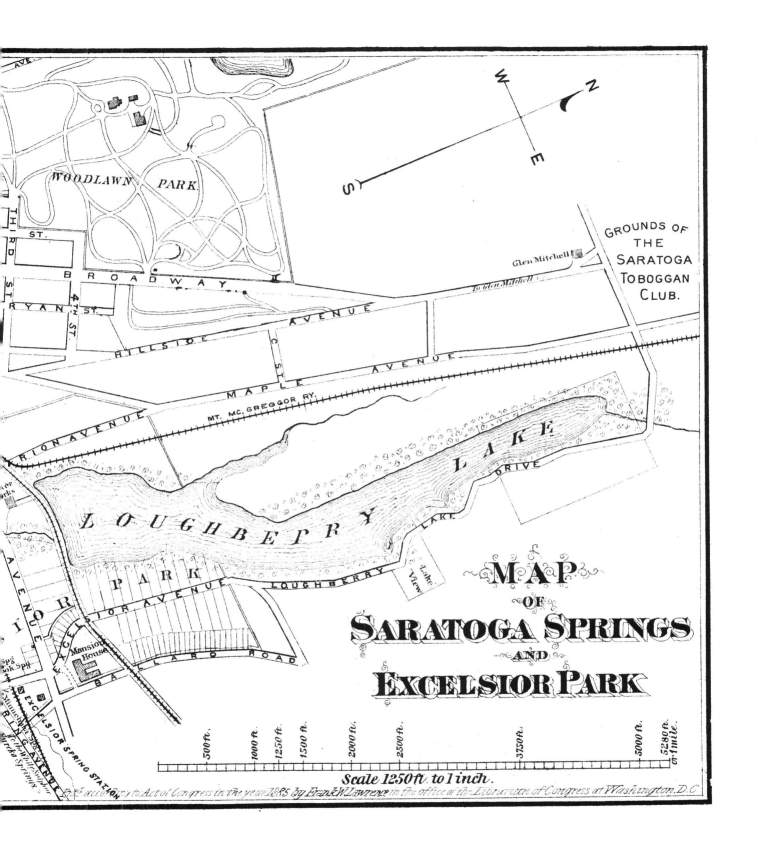

WOODLAWN PARK.

GROUNDS OF THE SARATOGA TOBOGGAN CLUB.

Glen Mitchell

To Glen Mitchell

THIRD ST.

RYAN ST.

4TH ST.

BROADWAY

HILLSIDE AVENUE

MAPLE AVENUE

MT. MC. GREGGOR RY.

ORION AVENUE

LOUGHBERRY LAKE

LAKE DRIVE

LOUGHBERRY

PARK

EXCELSIOR AVENUE

Lake View

...IOR AVENUE

EXCELSIOR AVENUE

Mansion House

BALLARD ROAD

EXCELSIOR SPRING STATION

EXCELSIOR SPRING AVENUE

MAP
OF
SARATOGA SPRINGS
AND
EXCELSIOR PARK

500 ft. | 1000 ft. | 1250 ft. | 1500 ft. | 2000 ft. | 2500 ft. | 3750 ft. | 5000 ft. | 5280 ft. or 1 mile.

Scale 1250 ft. to 1 inch.

FOREWORD

I fell in love with Saratoga Springs when I first saw it on a cold wintry day nearly forty years ago. I was newly wed to Cornelius Vanderbilt Whitney. He brought me there to spend the day and to see "Cady Hill House", the family summer residence. The inside of the house had no heat and was shivery cold, but the outside seemed to glow and beckon to me. I knew then, that it would be a place full of happiness for us, and for my five children.

We had lunch at the Gideon Putnam where Monty Wooley and his brother greeted us. Frank Sullivan soon arrived and it was like the "Round Table" in New York. The only person missing was Alexander Woolcott. I was so enchanted by this illustrious group that we stayed for the week, rather than the intended day! I needed to buy clothes for my extended visit, and was disappointed to find so many empty shops on Broadway. This saddened me immensely,

and I decided to try and find out more about this famous spa city. I bought every book I could find on the history of Saratoga Springs, and read with amazement of its opulence from the gay 1890s up until World War II. The Vanderbilts and Whitneys, both, played an enormous role in all of the social events in those days, and it was then that I promised my husband that I would try to help restore those grand old times!

With *Saratoga Lost*, Robert Joki helps preserve an important chapter in the history of 19th-century Saratoga Springs. The golden days of the grand Victorian era are restored in the pages of this book and come to life again before the very eyes of the modern reader, just as they were captured in time more than a century and a quarter ago by pioneering photographers.

Marylou Whitney
Cady Hill House
March, 1998

ACKNOWLEDGMENTS

Inspiration and support for this project came from numerous people and organizations. My apologies to the many not listed here who have nonetheless helped make this book possible.

I thank my parents for instilling in me a natural curiosity and interest in history, antiques and old photographs. Although they never directed me along these lines, they provided experiences which fostered my almost life-long pursuit.

The members of the National Stereoscopic Association have been instrumental in helping me put my photography collection together. This group of collectors and scholars regularly share information through a periodic magazine and actively trade and sell photographic views to each other. Many people throughout the country helped me form my collection, and I thank them all.

Rusty Norton of New Haven, Connecticut, has been a friend and occasional supplier of views for over twenty years now. Rusty is widely recognized for his knowledge of early photography. Throughout the world, museums, universities and individual collectors like myself seek him out for his knowledge and the great views he always manages to come up with.

The Saratoga Bottle Collectors Society has provided me with valuable information since its establishment in 1981. This nationwide group of bottle collectors goes far beyond just collecting old glass containers. They enthusiastically pursue the history of the mineral spring companies, collect related ephemera and readily share this information through a newsletter and at meetings.

Collectors Bill Grande and Minnie Bolster merit special attention. I've known both for many years, and each has a wonderful collection of Saratoga's past. Both have readily shared their knowledge and treasures.

Historians Martha Stonequist and Beatrice Sweeney are to be thanked. Martha works diligently, collecting and maintaining information in her capacity as current City Historian. I am especially indebted to her for the time and energy she spent reviewing a very rough draft of my book. I find evidence of Bea Sweeney's scholarly pursuits almost everywhere. We all know much more about Saratoga's past, and

have access to it, because of the admirable work she did at the City Historian's office and with the Historical Society.

Many others have played a part. John DeMarco at the Lyrical Ballad Bookstore long ago encouraged me to prepare a book from my collection. Field Horne, a respected historian at the National Museum of Racing and an enthusiastic student of Saratoga's past, also lent support. Ed Hotaling's well-researched book *They're Off* is so much more than just a history of the race course. His lively account of Saratoga's history includes a great deal of long-forgotten, but important, information about the community. Bernard Puckhaber's book on the region's mineral water bottles, *Saratogas*, is one that I have turned to often, and one which guided my initial interest in the mineral springs.

I have a great deal of admiration for Saratogians who long ago gathered, recorded and shared information about the past. Without their efforts, much of what we know would probably have been lost. Nathaniel Sylvester, Cornelius Durkee, Edmund Huling, William Stone, and Daniel Benedict come immediately to mind, but others recorded bits and pieces which now document the past.

The 19th-century photographers who captured the images included in this book merit special praise. Without their enterprise and hard work, this book would not exist.

I especially appreciate the help given by Jean Stamm and Ellen deLalla of the Saratoga Room in the Saratoga Springs Public Library. The library's Saratoga Room has a fine collection of historic material, and the staff and volunteers make this tremendous asset readily available to the community.

The Historical Society of Saratoga Springs is another valuable asset of the community. I thank John McKee and Gordon Harrower for their willing assistance in making the Society's resources available to me.

Thanks to Deborah Allen and Black Dome Press, my publishers. Without their willingness to take on this project, and their assistance in putting it together, this book would not be available today. I wish to thank Patricia Davis, Matina Billias, Ken Burrows and Steve Hoare for their help in proofreading the manuscript.

Special thanks to Marylou Whitney, surely Saratoga's most notable resident and civic supporter, for the kind words in the foreword.

Finally, more than anyone, I'd like to thank my wife, Susan, and my children, Sara and Todd. They supported me from the beginning and gave me plenty of time and patience to work on this project. For over twenty years, Susan has encouraged me to collect anything I thought was interesting or important, having the confidence that what I was pursuing was worthy. Many years ago, she suggested I do a book from my collection. My interest in history has rubbed off on the kids, but I know I've taxed their patience as they were "forced" to listen to yet another newly-discovered story about old Saratoga. My dream of publishing a book is now a reality, due in large measure to the support of my family.

INTRODUCTION

Beginning in the late 18th century and continuing throughout the 19th, visitors journeyed in great numbers to northern New York State to experience the celebrated watering place called Saratoga Springs. Located in the upper Hudson River lowlands, near the southeastern edge of the Adirondack Mountains, the small rural village was known far and wide for natural wonders found nowhere else in the new country. A special combination of circumstances in nature had blessed the Saratoga region with numerous medicinal mineral springs. Visitors, eager to benefit from these bubbling springs, were lured to the village to bathe in and drink the water.

The beginnings of this "lure of Saratoga" can be traced to the late 18th century when a community began to form in the vicinity of the mineral springs. During the 19th century the village flourished, attracting ever-increasing numbers of travelers, climaxing in the post-Civil War Victorian era. Although initially drawn by the mineral springs, the crowds were later enticed by the exciting social life and entertainment offered in and around this small village. Guests stayed in magnificent hotels and boarding houses, enjoying sumptuous feasts in fine dining rooms. Endless miles of piazzas and porches were packed with well-heeled tourists who, as part of their daily routine, formed a never-ending morning procession to the springs for a glass of bubbling water. These visitors took home notions and souvenirs purchased from an interesting assortment of shops and peddlers on and off Saratoga's Broadway. Many posed for photographers working an active trade in the village and purchased family portraits. Others took home scenic views to remember their stay. The photographer's camera would immortalize this Saratoga scene for future generations.

The pages which follow are illustrated by wonderful scenes of Saratoga's 19th-century past. They are scenes that an active imagination would be hard-pressed to create, and mere words are not enough to adequately describe or explain. These scenes capture glimmering fleeting moments in Saratoga's Victorian heyday in which health- and pleasure-seekers had their water, and had their fun. The photographs depict some, but certainly not all, of the hotels, springs and sights around Saratoga. There were many small boarding houses, businesses, residential neighborhoods and streets which were never captured by a photographer of the era.

Present-day Saratoga Springs is still deeply rooted in its Victorian past, and much of its charm stems from that colorful era. Unfortunately, most of the buildings pictured have disappeared. Many were removed from the scene when economic decline led to their demolition; others succumbed to fire and neglect. The crowds still come, and there are still many fine examples of architecture in the city, but what remains, particularly of the hotels and mineral spring pavilions, pales in comparison to what once was the pride and glory of Saratoga. Historic preservation efforts took place in a systematic and community-wide manner only after much of Saratoga's heritage already had been lost. Regrettably, precious little of this lost Saratoga remains alive in visual or written records.

The Civil War and Victorian years—1860 through the 1890s—brought unprecedented change and growth, and came to define the grand era of Saratoga. Fortunately, many skilled photographers worked the Saratoga trade recording this rich and colorful history. As your eyes wander over these pages, bear in mind the time frame; some things which are now considered quite old, antique and historic may not even have existed when these pictures were taken. So don't look for the old trolley station or drink hall, Model T Fords, the Spirit of Life Statue, Canfield's version of the Casino with its ballroom and leaded glass panels, the Italian Gardens and Fountains. You won't find the Adirondack Trust Bank, the old post office or Arcade Building, the Saratoga Spa State Park and its aging Roosevelt, Washington and Lincoln bathhouses. The pictures in this book are from an earlier time.

Throughout these pages, virtually no mention is made of the modern commercial buildings, homes, fields, roads and parking lots which now, at the end of the 20th century, occupy these sites. I prefer that the 19th century be viewed unencumbered by references to the 20th. It is distracting to gaze at an old photo of a piazza filled with hotel guests and have to think about a parking lot or some unremarkable modern edifice which now occupies its site. A brief explanation of what happened to these landmarks of Victorian architecture is, however, included in Chapter 9.

The high life of the post-Civil War years has often overshadowed and obscured what Saratoga Springs was really like for many visitors and residents. The annual Saratoga horse-racing meet was the only regularly recurring organized entertainment at the time and, as such, newspapers paid close attention to it and to the actions of the wealthy and flamboyant who patronized the races. It was good press, and it sold newspapers. The result is the misconception by many that just about the only explanation for the phenomenon of Saratoga and the Saratoga summer season was racing, gambling and the perpetual party life. The mineral springs, other time-honored attractions and entertainments, and the life of the local residents have been relegated to the background or even to obscurity. The fact is, Saratoga was a year-round community with activities occurring throughout all four seasons. The springs, shops, colorful amusements, and day-to-day activities of the local residents were all-important components of the Saratoga scene.

TERMINOLOGY AND
ARCHITECTURAL STYLES

The proper name of the village is, of course, Saratoga Springs, but I frequently refer to it as "Saratoga" or simply "the Springs." The three names have been in common usage for the last 150 years or more. When this area was first being explored, it was referred to simply as "the springs near Saratoga." The original Saratoga was the much older settlement now known as Schuylerville, or Old Saratoga.

The terms "Victorian" and "Victorian period" are derived from Queen Victoria's reign in England spanning the years 1837 to 1901. In everyday usage, the term "Victorian" is most frequently used in describing design or style in architecture, furniture and other decorative arts. Evidence of the influences of this period can be found throughout Saratoga. In the United States, the Early Victorian era begins about 1840 and is characterized stylistically by the Gothic Revival and the Italian Villa design. The High Victorian era spans 1865 to 1875 with a continuation of the Italian Style and its sub-categories, as well as the French Renaissance Revival (or so-called Mansard Style). Saratoga has many fine examples from this period. Finally, Late Victorian dates after 1875 and is made up stylistically of the Romanesque Revival and Queen Anne. Overlap and style-mixing often occurred, and many sub-categories and additional style designations exist. Because of the overlap, the dates should not be viewed as etched in stone. For the purposes of the text which follows, the generic term "Victorian" will apply to the entire period 1860-1899, and the use of "High Victorian" will refer specifically to the 10-15 year period following the Civil War (1865 through the 1870s).

MINERAL WATER

Saratoga Springs has long been known as "the great watering place." The reasons people bathe in and drink the water are varied, and the expected benefits numerous. This book is not a medical treatise. No attempt has been made to explain the properties and chemical compounds of each spring. Suffice to say that the waters were, and are, consumed both as medicine and beverage, and bathed in for the comfort and healing they bestow.

Notwithstanding the above, perhaps the one property the reader needs to know about the mineral springs regards their sulphur content. Today, just as in the past, there is confusion about this, caused undoubtedly by the smell and the taste. Saratoga's commercial mineral water springs are not sulphur springs, like those encountered so often around the country when drilling for well water. The mineral content of Saratoga's water is varied, and it is charged with carbonic acid gas which gives the water its bubbles. If any sulphur is contained in the mineral spring water, the quantity is minute and merely incidental to the other, more important, ingredients which give each water its unique properties. Obvious exceptions to this are the two White Sulphur Springs noted elsewhere in this book.

NINETEENTH-CENTURY PHOTOGRAPHY

Almost all photographs taken during the 1860s, 1870s and 1880s were the work of professional photographers, because affordable easy-to-use cameras were not yet available to the public. From the very beginning of the photographic trade, around 1840, the crowds and wealth of Saratoga drew many practitioners of the art. In the early years, they were limited primarily to portraiture, but scenic photographs became readily available and affordable with the advent of wet plate photography. The negative/positive system, and albumen prints with their characteristic brown tones, became the industry standard by 1860. The process was cumbersome and time-consuming, but allowed for the manufacture of multiple copies. Business boomed in Saratoga. Some enterprising photographers set up year-round studios and worked both the local and tourist trade. The firm of Baker and Record was the most active and prolific during the 1870s, producing many stunning and important views. The summer seasons also attracted photo-artists who set up temporary summer shops. Still others arrived, took a handful of plates, and then left. Views of Saratoga could be marketed almost anywhere.

Stereo photographs were the most common form of scenic view. By 1860, the hand-held stereoscope had been invented, and stereoscopic views were enthusiastically sought by those who could afford them. There was a worldwide fascination with the unique way in which they captured everything in 3D. People could sit on their porches or in their parlors and experience battles of the Civil War, see government buildings in Washington, view the ruins of ancient Egypt ... or gaze at the village in upstate New York so well known for its gay life and mineral springs. At Saratoga, tens of thousands of images were recorded in stereo over these years. Visitors eagerly purchased them to remember their stay or to carry away some cherished moment. Far beyond Saratoga, one could find bookstores and photo sellers in Boston, San Francisco or London offering views of Saratoga on hand, or available through catalogs. Large publishing firms produced wonderful sets. The largest firm at the time, E. & H.T. Anthony from New York City, marketed two series of Saratoga, including an extraordinary series of 59 views in 1865. Beer Brothers, a small New York City firm, published 92 views during the early years of the Civil War.

The wet plate camera prevailed until around 1880, when the dry plate began to make the job much easier. But professionals continued to be the only ones taking images, and most of them took pictures only of what they got paid to photograph, or of what they were likely to sell. A decade later, George Eastman was busy marketing an easy-to-use affordable camera. As the century was about to end, suddenly it seemed everybody was now taking pictures important to him or her. Neglected out-of-the-way places and residential neighborhoods finally had their chance.

The inherent technological limitations of early photography should be considered when studying old photographs. The era of wet plate cameras and long exposure times created images which are a far cry from those produced by modern high-speed shutters and the seemingly infinite variety of films. A long exposure time meant people had to patiently hold still to prevent the image from blurring, a problem which was most troubling when taking a group shot. Some scenes show "ghost figures"—an indistinct or faint image resulting when a person, or perhaps a horse and buggy, lingered in a scene long enough to have a partial image recorded, but not long enough to be fully discernible. Truly instantaneous photos were not generally possible until the 1880s. Photographers often worked early in the day or off-season so they could take views with a minimal amount of activity in the scene. Night scenes are very rarely encountered, and although interior shots were taken, they seldom show large groups of people. Pictures of Saratoga's grand balls, or of crowds in the dining halls in village hotels, would have been almost impossible to capture on a negative wet plate because of all the activity inherent in such scenes.

Finally, the physical environment itself limited what the photographer could shoot. For example, many hotels were much too large to capture in one photograph. Trees, leaves and other buildings often prevented a clear open image of the scene. The crowded confines of the small village streets frequently meant no vantage point was available for a good unobstructed picture.

AUTHOR'S COLLECTION—
PHOTOGRAPHS AND ILLUSTRATIONS

All photographs and ephemera used in this book are from my personal collection and represent but a small portion of it, acquired over a twenty-year period, mostly a few pieces at a time. They were gathered from dealers and collectors at antique shows, shops and flea markets; they came from attics and basements and in packages sent from other collectors across the country. The graphics and advertising illustrations come primarily from period guidebooks, village directories and related ephemera. They represent actual companies doing business in Saratoga during the Victorian years. Only a very few of the photographs herein have ever before been published in book form. Many are believed to be unique examples, and none has been retouched. Time has taken its toll on some of the photos, but I prefer to show them as they are.

Almost all photographs in this book are from original period stereoviews. Small-town America was widely photographed with stereo cameras in the 1860s, '70s and '80s, a time which coincides with Saratoga's grandest era. This fortunate coincidence, along with my wish to share these wonderful photographs with the public, has made this book possible. I welcome you to enjoy these captured moments of Saratoga's distant past.

4 Columbian Spring, Saratoga.

CHAPTER 1
HISTORICAL OVERVIEW

To understand and appreciate the importance of Saratoga Springs in the Victorian era, the reader must look back at its history. In barely a hundred years, what had once been wilderness had become one of the liveliest and best-known resorts in America—a remarkable feat for a small and somewhat isolated place to achieve. Saratoga Springs of 1875 was certainly not the Saratoga of 1775, but neither was it the Saratoga of 1830 or 1860 for that matter. Victorian Saratoga was a unique historical product of community and environment.

DISCOVERY

Legend and local lore account nearly as much as fact for the early days of Saratoga, since precious few records exist. The recorded history of Saratoga Springs begins with the discovery of High Rock Spring in the second half of the 18th century. Sir William Johnson, Superintendent of Indian Affairs in North America for the British Crown, is popularly regarded as the first white visitor, brought here by the Iroquois in 1771. The Iroquois had long admired and respected Johnson, and when he fell ill that year, they carried him through the wilderness to a curious mineral deposit and spring. Johnson drank their cherished medicine and bathed in the cool soothing liquid.

The Saratoga region, and High Rock Spring in particular, had been well known to native people for untold generations before. They were drawn by the healing water of the "medicine spring of the Great Spirit", as the Iroquois called the High Rock, and the abundant game found in the wilderness.

In the years after the American Revolution, word spread quickly across the country praising the region's mineral water, abundant timber and other natural resources. Small huts and shelters, and then cabins, were built by the earliest pioneers. Crude bath facilities were created to allow eager visitors the opportunity to benefit from nature's medicine flowing from the mineral cone and from a few other sources soon discovered nearby. Among the early visitors was General Philip Schuyler, who carved a path through the wilderness along Fish Creek from Schuylerville (then called Saratoga). High Rock was thereby connected to the Hudson River and to Schuyler's country home and mills at the old Revolutionary War battle site. The trail Schuyler blazed in 1783 became the first route providing "convenient" access to the springs, though travelers would still worry about bears, wolves and the great cats which roamed the swamps and dense forest along the way.

General George Washington visited High Rock Spring while inspecting military sites in the northeast. Accompanied by New York Governor George Clinton and Alexander Hamilton on the 1783 visit, Washington was impressed with the spring and even inquired about purchasing property in the area. He was unable to secure any, however, and later generations would look back and always wonder what would have become of Saratoga, indeed the country, if the General had been able to purchase land here.

While the land around High Rock Spring was the focus of the earliest development, an important new chapter in Saratoga's history began in the summer of 1792. Historical accounts tell of a small group setting out that summer to hunt game in the deep woods south of the mineral cone when one of their members, Nicholas Gilman, a congressman from New Hampshire, spotted clear water bubbling up from the ground. Word of a new mineral spring spread quickly, and it became known as Congress Spring in honor of its discoverer. The water was proclaimed superior to the other known sources and early travelers began to seek it out. Saratoga had a new "lure."

A COMMUNITY DEVELOPS

Congress Spring and a large tract of land surrounding it was eventually leased by the pioneer destined to become Saratoga's most ambitious and successful early developer. Gideon Putnam and his wife Doanda came to the area in 1789, initially settling near High Rock. Putnam's principal interest in the region was lumbering the ancient forest, producing wood staves and shingles. As he gained wealth, Putnam secured additional land and began to consider a new endeavor in the area about Congress Spring. In 1802, Putnam purchased a small parcel of land across from the now well-known spring and built a hotel, Saratoga's first, which he called Putnam's Tavern and Boarding House. Erected close to Congress Spring, which visitors were allowed to use free of charge, the accommodations were sorely needed, for visitors had long complained about the primitive accommodations at the spring. Although some considered it a folly to erect such a large hotel in the wilderness, Putnam's venture proved very successful.

With additional land purchased over the following years, Putnam began to lay out the surrounding area for development. He plotted a wide thoroughfare through his planned village and named it Broad Street. Elm trees planted along the street would one day grow tall and provide the village with a beautiful green canopy. Putnam's street would be known around the world in the Victorian years as Broadway, Saratoga Springs.

As land was cleared and the settlement near Congress Spring grew, Putnam discovered more mineral springs in the vicinity, which attracted even more visitors. In 1811, while constructing a larger and more beautiful second hotel to serve the gathering crowds, Putnam was injured in a fall. He never fully recovered, and died the following year before the hotel, Congress Hall, was completed. Doanda and their children carried on, eventually renaming their first hotel Union Hall. Congress Hall was taken over by a new owner, Guert Van Schoonhoven, and, when completed, the handsome structure was the finest in Saratoga. The Hall's front was 140 feet long and it had a small wing at its south end facing Congress Spring. Tall columns supported a sheltering roof across its front, just as at Union Hall across Broad Street. The pleasant piazzas would become an essential architectural feature of each of Saratoga's hotels. The elegant Congress became "the" place for the fashionable and wealthy during the summer season. To keep its guests entertained, the Hall employed a band and scheduled dances and balls on a regular basis during the season. It was the first Saratoga hotel to do so, and the practice became so popular other village hotels would soon follow suit.

During the years of early settlement, the area around Putnam's small development was known locally as the "lower village." The community forming around the High Rock was called the "upper village." In 1810, almost a mile of forest and swampy valley separated the two, which consisted of merely a couple dozen buildings each. But with rapid growth in the vicinity in the ensuing years, the town of Saratoga Springs was established in 1819. The Village of Saratoga Springs was officially incorporated in 1826, combining what had long been known as the upper and lower villages.

The fortunes of Saratoga Springs took a significant turn when Dr. John Clarke arrived on the scene at Congress Spring in 1823. A New York City soda fountain owner, Clarke recognized tremendous potential in the mineral water business. Though the water was given away freely at the spring's source, Clarke believed a good income could be derived from the sale of bottled water. Clarke was joined by Thomas Lynch, an associate from New York City, and together they began to market bottled Congress Water. Under the banner of Lynch and Clarke, they set about promoting the water throughout the country.

In 1826, Clarke finally established legal ownership of the celebrated spring (up to that point the spring itself was actually on public/common property). Clarke improved the property near the spring, ridding it of unsightly and unsanitary conditions. He cleared away unwanted brush and trees, filled in wet areas and created a drainage system to help dry up what had been a swampy basin. Aware of the commercial potential of drawing crowds to his spring, Clarke began to lay out park-like grounds and walkways around Congress and his nearby Columbian Spring. An aggressive and astute businessman, Clarke was soon able to establish Congress Water as the most widely-recognized mineral water in the country, and his park became an important part of the Saratoga scene. His success accounted for much of the fame of the developing village of Saratoga Springs, and his efforts helped insure Saratoga's place as the country's pre-eminent watering place, overcoming challenges from nearby Ballston Springs which during the first three decades of the 19th century had actually led Saratoga Springs in development.

At the same time Clarke began developing his Congress Water business, Elias Benedict and John Ford were busy working on a new brick landmark for Broad Street. Its cornerstone was set in 1823, and the following summer Saratoga's new fashionable place to spend the season was the United States Hotel. The handsome towering hotel stood four stories high, and its Broadway piazza provided a pleasant vista of the crowds and carriages passing through the village. Although "the States" drew some patrons away from the older Union and Congress Halls, and another well-known hotel of that period, the Pavilion, there were plenty of new visitors arriving each summer, and each house continued to grow and prosper. By 1830, under James Marvin's ownership, an enlarged United States could accommodate 200 guests (another source suggests 300), and "Saratoga's pride" was said to be one of the most splendid edifices in the entire nation.

Saratoga's springs and hotels were already attracting a crowd of rich and famous by the 1820s. Joseph Bonaparte was one of the more colorful. The brother of Napoleon and a former king of Spain, Joseph was so taken by the area that he, like George Washington before him, attempted to purchase land, and, like Washington, his attempts also failed, despite a very generous offer to one landholder. Bonaparte settled elsewhere and bore no grudge, making a number of return trips to the Springs in the years to follow.

TRANSPORTATION

While the village grew in the 1820s, one significant problem which hampered its settlement and expansion was the fact that it was far from the main population centers of the country. A trip to the Springs in the early 1800s usually meant a long, time-consuming, arduous journey. From distant destinations, many travelers began their journey aboard ships working the Atlantic coast. At New York City and other ports in the northeast, more passengers joined them, usually taking a sloop or steamship up the Hudson River to Albany or Troy, though others traveled the entire way by horse-drawn carriage. All travelers had to rely on horse and coach for the final leg of the journey, traveling over the rough, dusty, and occasionally muddy roads crossing the county. The trek became more tolerable after 1823 when the Champlain Canal linked Waterford, just north of Albany, with Schuylerville. The canal packets were slow-moving, but much more comfortable than horse and coach. Some travelers came to prefer this route but, for the most part, the canal boats were used primarily to ferry goods.

This long and tiring journey became more bearable and less time-consuming in 1832 when a railroad line, one of the nation's first, was laid to the village from Schenectady. Initially, horses pulled carriages set upon the rails, their trip interrupted by a stream crossing north of Ballston Spa (formerly called Ballston Springs) which was not yet complete. By the summer of 1833, the first locomotive was placed upon the Saratoga and Schenectady Railroad, and the direct link was finished. The faster and more efficient train soon became the preferred route and helped insure Saratoga's accessibility. By the summer of 1836, passengers boarding in New York City accomplished the trip in a mere 16 to 18 hours. With additional rail lines added during the following decades, Saratoga's ability to attract visitors was further enhanced. Steamship and rail lines meant people from around the world could "conveniently" visit the Springs, and a marked increase in tourist travel encouraged commercial growth throughout the village.

ARISTOCRATIC ERA: 1830-1860

In the years prior to the Civil War, many of Saratoga's guests traveled great distances primarily for the relaxation and therapy the spa offered. They came from everywhere across the nation, among them numerous wealthy travelers who made the long trek northward from the old South to escape the heat of summer. Some visitors were sick or invalids who came with their families in the hope that the precious waters would cure their ills. Their summer sojourn was not merely a vacation; these were medical and restful retreats. During these years generally characterized by a refined social scene, other guests began to seek the "excitement" at Saratoga. The village was growing, and small inns, boarding houses and taverns were replaced by much larger and more elegant hotels. The most famous grew dramatically. The United States and the Union each would eventually number over 500 rooms just prior to the Civil War. Architectural styles came to reflect a new era as classic Federal gave way to Greek Revival, and then to early Victorian forms. Picturesque pavilions and small bathhouses were built at the most promising springs as owners sought to give their water recognition and importance. The most celebrated waters were commercially developed, and a few, like the Empire and Pavilion Springs, were bottled and sent to distant markets, just like Congress water. In ritual fashion, crowds gathered at each spring each morning. Taking a glass of healing water in the early hours of the day became a practice followed by all travelers.

But Saratogians realized they had to offer more than just mineral water and baths if the community were to continue to prosper. Saratoga needed recreation and excitement to keep the visitors coming. After all, the morning procession and a daily mineral bath occupied no more than a few hours of the day. Lawn games, carriage rides, picnicking, and boating upon Saratoga Lake became popular and restful pursuits. Religious meetings, debates, public lectures and musical concerts were organized. During this period, 1830-1860, popularly known as Saratoga's elegant "Aristocratic Era," many of the nation's "old wealth" and social aristocracy spent their summers at the Springs. The genteel and refined life beckoned to many important national and international literary, religious, business and political figures.

To characterize the times solely as "the Aristocratic Era" is, however, a bit of a misnomer. Overall, the atmosphere of the village was refined, but there were abundant opportunities to pursue all manner of physical and social pleasures. The independent American spirit demanded new offerings. In the great hotel ballrooms, wealthy fashionable young gentlemen and ladies danced and partied to a brisk, livelier tune at their cotillion parties. A new dance party, termed the "hop", became a highly popular evening activity, adding both pleasure and notoriety to the Saratoga social scene. Along Broadway, enterprising Saratoga merchants catered to consuming visitors. Itinerant peddlers added color and curiosity, as they too sought cash from the summer trade. Travelers had no trouble finding card games, liquor, billiards, shooting galleries, and almost anything else money could buy at the time. Not unexpectedly, as any place that drew crowds and wealth also attracted less desirable elements, gamblers and hustlers, looking to make a quick easy dollar, made their way to Saratoga along with the more refined set.

Sporting and special events also became a popular part of the Saratoga scene, including America's favorite sport of the era, horse racing. A trotting course began holding races outside of the village, on East Congress Street, in the summer of 1847. The small track, destined to be called Horse Haven

on Union Avenue, drew Lady Suffolk, the original "Old Grey Mare," to compete in its first, and well-attended, meet. A month later, in September, former presidents Martin Van Buren and John Tyler, along with future president Millard Fillmore and statesman Daniel Webster, were in town to visit the New York State Agricultural Fair held on property near the new track. P.T. Barnum and General Tom Thumb were on the scene to cash in on the gathering crowds.

As time passed, this ever-increasing array of entertainment and amusement became Saratoga's new summer drawing card. The staid and refined life of an earlier time began to take a back seat to the fun-filled gaiety of a new age, though the mineral springs continued to be the foundation upon which the community existed. The changing social scene meant some so-called aristocrats and elitists ceased coming to Saratoga. One proper Englishman's impression of the changing scene was summarized as follows: "For a time the select had it all to themselves, but by-and-by everybody began to resort to it, and on everybody making his appearance the select began to drop off, and what was once very genteel is now running the risk of becoming exceedingly vulgar."[1] With the outbreak of the Civil War, wealthy southerners, who had long patronized the springs, also saw their summer sojourns come to an end.

CIVIL WAR AND POST-CIVIL WAR VICTORIAN ERA: 1860-1890

Nationwide, the consuming concern of the 1860s was the Civil War and its aftermath. Residents of Saratoga closely followed the course of the war, and many of its citizens patriotically joined the effort to preserve the Union. The war raged on for four years, and many local men gave their lives for the cause, yet the economic and social fabric of the village held together, barely interrupted by the struggle and suffering. Buildings were erected, springs were tubed and water exported, and guests continued to arrive in the summer months. A new attraction, the Saratoga Race Course, had its beginnings during the great conflict. Guided largely by Saratoga's wealthiest summer visitor, Commodore Vanderbilt, gambler John Morrissey launched a racing meet for thoroughbred horses in the summer of 1863. The success of the meet encouraged the creation of a new facility by the following summer.

But there was a cruel irony to those Civil War summers. While patriotic Saratogians were on the battlefields giving their all and longing to be back home, wealthy and influential young summer guests, some of whom had bought their way out of the conflict, were safe from harm, enjoying the good life in Saratoga. Saratoga endured, just as the nation would, and there was little indication at the time of the great changes that were in store for the village in the decades to come.

After the Civil War, pent-up energies were unleashed and a nationwide surge in railroad construction ensued, resulting in an unprecedented volume of summer visitors to Saratoga. These travelers, including many northerners possessing new-found wealth, were lured by the promise of wonderful experiences quite unlike anything found elsewhere in the country. An expanding post-war economy, and an era of rapid technological and industrial advances, had created a whole new class of wealthy Americans. In 1850, there were, perhaps, twenty millionaires in the entire country, but by 1890 their numbers would swell to over 4000. The village eagerly opened its doors to offer the excitement and good times the newly-rich wanted, thus swelling the coffers of local businesses. The expansion of summer travel firmly established Saratoga as the north's most popular social resort, and the village justly bore the title "Queen of Spas."

The style and spirit of the High Victorian era in the postwar years was pervasive nationwide, profoundly influencing almost all aspects of life. People across the country turned to new styles and trends to put the agonizing war behind them and relieve the tedium of bygone days. Perhaps the most obvious outward expression of this was in the art and architecture which graced the homes and communities of America.

Caught up in this change, Saratoga started taking on a more fanciful, exhibitionist appearance. A new era with its new wealth was on full display, boldly proclaimed by opulent, lavishly-decorated buildings and fashionable events. Bordering the streets, grand and beautiful Victorian structures now welcomed the seasonal crowds. Along Broadway, commercial blocks offered a variety of "fancy goods" and treasures usually found only in the likes of New York City and Paris. Despite the village's small size, Saratoga became the proud home of some of the nation's largest and most extravagant hotels. Accommodations had always been one of the community's most distinctive and well-known features, but

during the 1870s the offerings grew to phenomenal proportions. The best known houses were the forever-expanding "new Victorian" Grand Union Hotel, and the recently-rebuilt High Victorian reincarnations of the United States Hotel and Congress Hall. Among the three great houses, over 5000 guests could stay in comfort and splendor.

Forsaking the genteel habits of an earlier time, guests took part in the impressive spectacle. They donned the latest and most stylish fashions and paraded around the village in all their finery. Fancy hops, festive parties and grand balls topped off the scene. Thoroughbred horse racing at the new Saratoga Race Course and gambling became well-attended and highly-publicized entertainments. Wealthy visitors spent freely in plush gaming establishments, but residents with a few silver dollars in their pockets found action as well in the saloons and taverns about the town. Even though gambling had always been illegal, gaming houses flourished and were kept in operation by occasional "gifts" to community organizations and local officials. Reformists decried the illegal vice, but gambling continued because of the economic benefits it brought to some residents who gained from rents, employment, and the sale of a host of goods and services needed to keep the gambling houses going.

During the Victorian summer seasons, Saratoga became well known for its parade of rich and famous in all their pomp and splendor. Newspapers across the nation chronicled the activities, telling of the parties, culinary feasts, races, gambling, and wanton flaunting of money at the Springs. The wealthy, and an endless procession of "wannabe's" following closely on their heels, gave journalists a lot to write about. But Saratoga was also a community which readily welcomed patrons of lesser means. Unlike in other, more pretentious resorts, great wealth and social status were not requirements. For every Commodore Cornelius Vanderbilt and his offspring, for every Jay Gould, Alexander Stewart, Diamond Jim Brady and Lillian Russell, there were a thousand others who took the summer in Saratoga in more modest circumstances.

There was something special about Saratoga, something no other place in America could match. Mechanics, laborers, merchants, businessmen, panhandlers and dreamers, the sons and daughters of tycoons, and the leading wealth of the nation all crossed paths here during the summer months. It was the rich and famous whom the press followed, and who boarded and partied in luxury, but in reality, nowhere else in America was there such a diverse concentration of people from such varied economic and social backgrounds. Only on the sidewalks of Broadway or upon the porches of the grand hotels could the child of a launderer or teamster pass so openly among the nation's richest families.

Saratoga's year-round residents were a cross section of America. Perhaps partly for that reason, plus a willingness to please its guests, the village was more open and tolerant than other well-known Victorian resorts. The summer vacation was not yet a ritual of American life. Most people had neither the time—a six or seven-day work week was still common— nor the money. But local farmers, mill workers and shop clerks did venture forth from their nearby fields and factory towns to witness the spectacle at Saratoga. They could not participate by spending the season in the big hotels or attending the gala parties, but they could have an afternoon enjoying the festive Broadway promenade. They could take all the mineral water they wanted at the springs. They could pass an afternoon or evening at a political gathering or fraternal meeting, or be inspired by a church sermon delivered by a famous orator. They could enjoy the pageantry and fanfare of a festive circus parade, or a regimental procession along Broadway. Numerous small, modest boarding houses off Broadway provided plenty of affordable rooms for those who chose to stay overnight.

Throughout the 19th century, village life was largely ruled by the calendar and climate and followed recurring patterns. Summers were filled with crowds and gaiety, but given the harsh winters, comparatively little tourist activity went on outside of "the season." The big hotels closed, and few visitors trickled into the village. Many residents spent the rest of the year preparing for the next season. But, much like in other communities across America, a healthy local economy was sustained throughout the year, supported by all manner of trades and businesses from blacksmiths to lawyers, bricklayers to shopkeepers.

From each October to May, Saratoga was abuzz with workers constructing homes, hotels and storefronts, working in small factories, or laboring at the mineral water bottling houses. Individual projects could occupy hundreds of workers at a time, such as in the spring of 1876, when 375 toiled around the clock on a major expansion of the Grand Union Hotel. Meanwhile, another 175 were busy creating a new Congress Park, and over 100 more were putting the finishing touches on the new Windsor Hotel.

There were numerous year-round stores on Broadway and the side streets which catered to an ongoing trade. Entertainment and cultural pursuits continued throughout the year at the Town Hall, the churches, and the smaller year-round hotels. Traveling troupes and musical entertainment were frequent offerings. Horse racing was not limited just to the heat of summer. Well-attended matches, primarily trotting events, were held at a number of places around the village where racers sped along tracks of dirt, mud, frozen ground, snow and ice.

But it was through the ever-increasing summer crowds that Saratoga's fame and fortune was secured. There were, of course, ups and downs due to changing economic and social conditions, but they were merely occasional, temporary setbacks to a lively and vibrant, forward-looking village. Saratoga Springs was a village with greatness in its path. And there was an entire country full of people anxious to catch a glimpse of the things that made it so.

There was no characteristic Victorian summer visitor, nor is there one single answer to why they came, what they did while here, or what they saw. Saratoga meant different things to different people, and a wealth of offerings catered to their varied needs. The magic and excitement of Saratoga was for everyone to discover in his or her own unique way.

One visitors' guidebook of the period suggests that there were "really a half dozen different Saratogas", each of which attracted its own "set." The guidebook points out that "Here, young men come with fast teams and a keen interest in pretty faces and the races. Hither wend the fop and the flirt, whose paradise is the ballroom; this realm is ruled by the millionaire and the managing mother. Then too there is the Saratoga of the sportsman. Also a Saratoga of the invalid. Outside all of these Saratogas, there is still another, which attracts thousands of sensible, healthy, but busy and over-worked people, who come here every year for genuine recreation."[2]

What would these visitors find? What was waiting for them as they pulled into the station? What would they see, and what would they do?

Near the eastern edge of the State of New York, USA, and bordered by the Hudson and Mohawk Rivers, lies the ancient county of Saratoga, famous in history and in medical science for its battlefields and healing springs. The village of Saratoga Springs, in the center of the county, and the largest village in it, is known round the globe. Tens of thousands of the fashionable world annually visit this celebrated resort. ... In approaching Saratoga Springs, over two railways, either from the north or south, the traveler meets with a surprise. The change from farms to close built town is abrupt, and the cars are among the houses, and at the station, almost before the fields are missed. From the south, the first intimation is the little group of cottages, clustered about the Geyser Springs, perhaps 3 minutes before the train stops. From the north, the brand-new villas and embryo streets of

Excelsior Park, the towers and the mansard roofs of the great hotels, flash past just as the brakes begin to pull up for the depot. In either case the train slides along the same covered platform, and "Saratoga" is announced. The intelligent brakeman knows the station is really "Saratoga Springs," but, with that freedom for which he is famous, he clips the "Springs." Saratoga is quite another place. This is Saratoga Springs, properly called so. The long platform swarms with importunate hack-men, and, were it not for good policing, the arrival would be a trifle formidable. To find the porter of your house a glance at the row of signs overhead will show you just where the correct man stands, and where you should go to find him. Each hotel has a reliable man under its sign, and the badge on his hat will make the assurance sure. There is no need to hasten to secure rooms. This is the land of vast hotels, and a party of six or more is a small affair where twenty thousand people may be housed at once. Having found one's house, and a little leisure, it may be in order to look at the village. Saratoga Springs is a village of hotels and dwelling houses. There are few manufactories, and its streets seem devoted to elegant leisure or abundant shopping. The principal street is Broadway, extending a little east of north through the entire village, and making the grand drive and promenade, where all the life, business and pleasure of the place may be seen in a five minute's walk. This concentration of hotels and stores on one street, and in the immediate neighborhood of nearly all of the springs, gives the village a singular aspect; for, away from this center, there is nothing but houses and cottages, and villas, each in prim fashion facing its quiet, shady street, a village of homes. Broadway is peculiar and original. The hotels, the elegant stores, the fine rows of trees, the broad borders of sod, and the throng of carriages and people that crowd its walks and roads, present a spectacle unlike anything else in the world. Newport and Interlaken and Long Branch have their special charms, but nowhere is so much general splendor concentrated in so limited a space. No other resort can show two such palaces as the Grand Union and Congress Hall, facing each other on one street. Perhaps no other place would lug two such monster buildings into such pronounced rivalry. Be that as it may, here they stand, and the general effect is remarkable, and a trifle oppressive. There is too much architectural glory; but the American likes grandeur, and here he has it, in a profusion perfectly dazzling—certainly there is but one Saratoga in the world— five minutes' walk up or down Broadway, takes one past all the great houses and the best stores. Congress Park and its springs give a rural aspect to the avenue, and the stately rows of trees afford agreeable shade. The walks are good, and the road well kept. Thousands crowd the way in elegant attire and there is a world of faces and things to see and admire. The throng of carriages passes in brilliant procession, flowers and elegant drapery fill the windows and frame the faces looking out, making a bit of realistic fairy-land that wins the attention at every step. The numerous shade trees give the town the appearance of a very beautiful forest city. Away from Broadway one sees home-life, quiet or gay, sober or festive, in countless houses, stretching through well swept shady streets in endless variety. Round all is the charming open country, with woods, lakes and meadows and with mountain ranges to fringe the blue horizon. The houses are generally small, as if the house-keeper did not intend to be much cumbered with the cares of many rooms. Every house has its own garden, and grass is freely used as a general outdoor carpet and embroidery. Many of the houses are of brick, and all exhibit a refreshing freedom of design, as if the owners had their own ideas of comfort, and meant their homes to express themselves. If they do, the Saratogians are a goodly people, cleanly, hospitable, and agreeable. Everything is as neat as wax, and there is an air of elegant finish about the houses and gardens that is infinitely suggestive and comforting. The visitor at once concludes that a residence among such homes must be pleasant, and there he is certainly correct."[5]

RAILROAD STATION

Photographers—Baker and Record, Saratoga

Most Victorian visitors came to Saratoga Springs by train, arriving here at this handsome station with mansard roof and clock tower. Erected in 1871 to serve as the main passenger depot for the village, it was scene to a flurry of activity with each arriving train during the festive summer season. This depot replaced earlier versions built along Division Street just west of Broadway. As the years went by, the initial rail line from Schenectady to Saratoga had been joined by additional tracks heading to Rensselaer and Whitehall, making connections with boats on the Hudson River and Lake Champlain, as well as continuing with rail stops far beyond to the north and south. In time, routes also served other destinations, including the Adirondacks, Mt. McGregor, Saratoga Lake, Schuylerville, and beyond to New England. In this view, it is likely the station crew and baggage boys posed for local photographers Baker and Record. The firm carried on a brisk trade taking stereoscopic pictures around the village during the 1870s.

UNITED STATES HOTEL LIVERY,

RAILROAD ARCADE

Photographers—Baker and Record, Saratoga

Arriving passengers departed their trains on the right side of the depot arcade pictured here. With the village at hand, they were then whisked off to local destinations, ferried by carriages and baggage carriers lining up on the left. The arrival of each train brought business for the local liveries, some maintained by the village hotels, and others which were independently owned. Signs hung overhead in the ironwork advertised local businesses, hotels and boarding houses, and their porters met new arrivals under these signs.

DIVISION STREET
Photographers—Record and Epler, Saratoga

Coaches leaving the train station made their way along Division Street and headed to Saratoga's main thoroughfare, Broadway. In so doing, travelers were immediately confronted by the enormous scale of Saratoga's landmark buildings. In this early 1880s view, the United States Hotel on the left was one of the so-called "Big Three," while the Arlington on the right was a smaller, though popular, hostelry.

VIEW FROM TOP OF UNITED STATES HOTEL LOOKING SOUTH
Photographers—McDonnald and Sterry, Albany and Saratoga

Climbing onto the roof of the United States Hotel, photographers McDonnald and Sterry captured a scene occasionally enjoyed by the traveler, but seldom immortalized by a photograph in this early period. Iron-railed lookouts atop the largest hotels provided the means to gaze out over the panorama. The scene shows just how close the hotels were to each other, and how relatively small the village of Saratoga was compared to its renowned status. In this photo, showing the area south of the middle of the village, the upper floors of the Grand Union Hotel are seen on the right, while at the left is the top portion of Congress Hall. The large Queen Anne building in the distance is the Windsor Hotel. Hidden by the trees is the hustle and bustle that occupied Broadway below. Elms planted earlier in the century created a wonderful canopy for the thoroughfare.

STREET SCENE, COACH TRAFFIC

Photographers—Baker and Record, Saratoga

Surely the traveler's senses would be stirred by all the sights, sounds and smells created by this activity of man and beast. This mid-1870s scene attests to the problems on congested Broadway long before the coming days of the horseless carriage. Coaches fill the street between the well-known Congress Hall on the left, and the Grand Union Hotel which is just outside this scene on the right. At the hotels, guests secured transportation to places within the village and to destinations beyond, such as the Geysers and Saratoga Lake. Roads at this time were formed of crushed limestone and hardpacked dirt and rubble, which would often turn into mud when the rains came. Note the section of larger cobblestone in front of the Grand Union; it provided sure footing and a clean step when getting into the carriages, especially on rainy days.

Boots, Shoes and Rubbers

Of all Descriptions, at the Saratoga Boot & Shoe Store,
102 Broadway, Saratoga Springs, N. Y

BROADWAY LOOKING NORTH

Photographers—McDonnald and Sterry,
Albany and Saratoga

Another scene on Broadway, this one looking north just outside the entrance to Congress Park, shows the Civil War monument in its proud and prominent setting. The monument commemorates local citizenry who answered President Lincoln's call to preserve the Union—the 77th Regiment, NY Volunteer Infantry, the so-called "Bemis Heights Battalion." The monument was dedicated in September of 1875.

BROADWAY, SARATOGA

OVERVIEW SHOWING CONGRESS SPRING/ CONGRESS HALL/MORRISSEY'S CLUB HOUSE

Publisher—E. & H.T. Anthony, NYC

Within the area captured in this photo, countless visitors pursued health and happiness during the Saratoga summers. This lovely view was taken in the early 1870s from an upper floor of the Grand Central Hotel, a large and elegant hotel located on the west side of Broadway opposite the Congress Spring. The Congress pavilion, at the lower right, was one of Saratoga's most widely-recognized landmarks. Just to the left of the spring are buildings where Congress Water was bottled and packed for shipment throughout the country. The south tower of Congress Hall looms on the far left. Beyond the bottling plant are two buildings owned by well-known boxer, politician and gambler, John Morrissey. The brick building was his Club House, and the structure with the mansard roof in the middle of this view was another gambling house. No single scene could possibly contain more of the things which drew the seasonal visitor to Saratoga.

CONGRESS HALL

Publisher—E. & H.T. Anthony, NYC

Many a fortunate traveler called Congress Hall home during the summer season. This view shows it as it looked in the early 1870s, when it was one of the three largest hotels in the village. Fronting Broadway, and having the rooms to house 1500 guests, the Hall spanned the entire thoroughfare between Spring Street and the entrance to Congress Park. This building opened for business in 1868 after the original Congress Hall (dating back to Gideon Putnam's days) was destroyed by fire in May, 1866. The architecture reflects post-Civil War tastes, and exhibits much of the High Victorian adornment typical at the time.

PIAZZA CONGRESS HALL

Photographers—Baker and Record, Saratoga

Saratoga Springs became well known for its magnificent piazzas. Usually two or three stories high, and lined with countless rockers and chairs, they served as important gathering places. Friends and strangers would meet, gossip, listen to music, place and settle wagers, flirt, argue, fall in love, play cards or restfully pass the time away. From here, on the front piazza of Congress Hall, one could watch an endless spectacle on Broadway and ponder all the activity and magic this village had to offer.

VIEW LOOKING NORTH FROM
CORNER OF CONGRESS STREET
*Photographers—Baker and Record,
Saratoga*

Everywhere the traveler looked there was the splendor of a prosperous and enticing resort. Well known was the Grand Union Hotel on the left, and Congress Hall, only partially visible to the right.

Often unseen, but nonetheless appreciated by travelers and residents, was a vast infrastructure of new technologies which supported the village and provided for everyone's comfort. Transportation, communication, heat, light, water and waste disposal were all-important. A few noteworthy milestones mark the era.

A transportation system was essential, and throughout the 19th century horse-drawn coaches arrived from all directions. But it was the railroads which proved vital to attracting huge crowds.

In 1853, evenings and nights in the village became brighter when gas lights began to appear upon the scene.

Years later, in the summer of 1879, the commercial electric light bulb was introduced to the village. Over the ensuing years, lines distributed power throughout the village, and eventually the new bulbs replaced the old gas lamps.

The telegraph allowed outside communications when a line connected Saratoga with Troy in 1846. Communications took a step forward in 1877 as Saratoga became linked by telephone to Ballston Spa, Schuylerville and Troy. In 1882, the first Saratoga Telephone Exchange opened.

By the mid-1870s, a new main sewer through Spring Valley and its many feeder lines was washing away all of the waste from the hotels. Lines eventually reached throughout many residential neighborhoods. The waste flowed unseen in the buried ancient brook draining the greater Saratoga area.

Another important milestone was the establishment of a new village water supply in 1871, when Loughberry Water Works opened. Some places, like the Grand Union Hotel, nonetheless continued operating their own private water supplies.

Until the early 1870s, Saratogians warmed their homes and businesses almost exclusively with wood. Descriptions of Broadway in winter suggest it looked more like a wood lot than a vibrant commercial street. The coal business began to thrive in the mid-1870s as supplies became readily available at Schuylerville from barges at the Champlain Canal basin. Railroads soon joined in the trade, delivering to village coal yards.

Just as winter consumed one resource, it provided another. Ice for summer refrigeration was available at lakes Loughberry, Lonely and Saratoga. Many large hotels had their own ice houses nearby, while independent companies stored and sold ice to a wide market. Crews cut, hauled and stored large cakes throughout the cold season.

LOOKING NORTH UP BROADWAY FROM WINDSOR HOTEL.

Photographers—Baker and Record, Saratoga

The photographer pointed his camera north, looking up Broadway, and caught in time the Congress Hall on the right and the Grand Union Hotel on the left. The view was probably taken from an upper floor porch of the Windsor Hotel around 1880. On the right, at mid-distance, is the entrance to Congress Spring and Park; the vacant foreground awaits development, which took place a few years after this photo was taken.

"*Poster*"
464   KID   B'way
GLOVES
(PATENTED JUNE 13TH, 1876.)

STORES AT THE GRAND UNION HOTEL

Photographer—Rumsey Publisher—Edwards & Luce, Cortland, NY

Commerce carried on by village merchants insured that almost anything was available at the Springs, where well-heeled travelers spent freely. Pictured here, at the northern end of the Grand Union Hotel block, are stores offering "fancy goods." Dannenbaum proudly advertised imported French kid gloves, parasols, and sash ribbons, and the enticing scene surely lured many inquisitive tourists inside. The vast range of goods gave Saratoga an international flair, and such colorful scenes added much to the appeal and excitement of the village.

FRONT PIAZZA, GRAND CENTRAL HOTEL, GILMORE'S BOSTON BAND 4 PM
Publisher—Hall Brothers, Brooklyn, NY

Scenes such as this were often encountered in Victorian Saratoga. Here, on the front piazza of the Grand Central Hotel, Gilmore's Boston Band sat down for its four o'clock afternoon concert. Management of this large and wonderfully-decorated hotel provided musical entertainment for the guests, as did many other hotels in the village during the summer season. Most large hotels offered three concerts a day. The Grand Central opened for business in July, 1872, and provided three summers of fun and excitement before it was tragically consumed by fire.

COLEY'S OYSTER HOUSE/PUTNAM SPRING BATH

Photographer—unknown

Supported by the summer hotels and guests on Broadway, and by permanent residents throughout the year, were a host of small shops and businesses scattered around the village. Many were located just east of Broadway, in Spring Valley, on Phila, Caroline, Henry and Putnam Streets. There, cobblers, grocers, tailors, launderers, blacksmiths and carpenters set up shop and worked their trades. Coley's Oyster House was one such business during the Victorian era. It was only a few steps from Broadway, down Phila, and served as a restaurant and market. Oyster baskets set along the walk enticed passersby, while lobsters, fish and groceries were offered inside.

The awning and sign at right is from the Putnam Spring Mineral Bath. The spring was located behind this edifice and, during earlier times, a large bathhouse, dating back to 1837, stood nearby. The buildings seen here were razed in the early 1890s to make room for the elegant Saratoga Baths, which drew their bubbling water from the old Putnam, and their patrons from nearby Broadway.

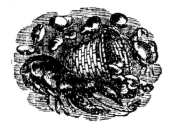

COLUMBIAN SPRING
Photographer—D. Barnum, Boston and Saratoga

Deloss Barnum was an enterprising photographer whose main studio was in Boston, but who spent considerable time in Saratoga Springs and other resorts serving a resident and tourist clientele. During the 1860s, he took many stereoscopic views in Saratoga, and in such diverse other places as the White Mountains, Niagara Falls, New York City and the small towns of New England. A master photographer, he is responsible for documenting many noteworthy gatherings in Saratoga. Most of his views are visually appealing, like this late-1860s view of the Columbian Spring, located only a few yards from its much more famous neighbor, Congress Spring. Barnum's busy summer studio was located just across Broadway from this site.

CARRIE KILMER AND ELIZABETH MCNUTT
Photographer—P.H. McKernon, Saratoga

The two young women are from prosperous local families engaged in the farm and lumber business. The Kilmers and McNutts lived near Middle Grove and, like other county residents, took occasional trips into Saratoga Springs to experience its pleasures and to shop at its stores.

SPRING VALLEY, HIGH ROCK SPRING AND BOTTLING HOUSE
Photographer—D. Barnum, Boston and Saratoga

The initial settlement of Saratoga Springs occurred here, in the area around the High Rock Spring. The historic High Rock mineral water fountain drew many inquisitive visitors, from Native Americans in prehistoric times, to wealthy travelers brought by private rail cars in the post-Civil War heyday. The environment pictured here changed many times over the years. In this view, the small mid-19th-century pond was formed in the spring valley by the village brook and a high water table. Maps of the 1850s, however, note that there had once been a large brickyard in this general area. Across from the pond is the High Rock Spring pavilion and bottling house, erected just after the Civil War. This view was probably taken shortly thereafter, since the scene changed again when the Seltzer Spring was tubed and a large brick bottling house was built next to the High Rock just before 1870.

The scene was one of on-going change: by 1876, the setting looked much different, as the pond had already been drained and filled in. That year, visitors had a new spring to sample, and soon a new bathhouse to enjoy along the old pond site. The spring had a unique ability to magnetize iron objects, and it was accordingly dubbed the Magnetic Spring. By 1881, the scene changed once more when the valley was pierced by a new railroad line heading from Lake Avenue through the valley and on to Saratoga Lake.

ENTRANCE TO WASHINGTON SPRING
Publisher—E. & H.T. Anthony, NYC

Heading south on Broadway just past the Congress Spring, tourists were welcomed by this lovely entrance to the Washington Spring and the Clarendon Hotel gardens. Like the other springs in the village, Washington's waters flowed free of charge here at the water's source. Dipper boys, working for tips, were stationed at most springs. Revenue for the spring owners was generated by the sale of water put up in bottles and kegs and delivered to area hotels, and to a wide market throughout the country and overseas.

LAKE IN GEYSER PARK

Photographers—Baker and Record, Saratoga

Rural scenes were always close by for the tourist who wanted to leave town. This picture shows a scene located about 1 1/2 miles south of the village hotels, on the way to Ballston Spa. A dam on the Coesa Creek created the small Coesa Lake, and during much of the 19th century this area was known as Ellis Corners. There were farms and a small mill built along the streambank, as well as a rural school, store and small hotel nearby. During the 1870s, spouting mineral fountains were discovered in this area, which led to increased development and a flood of tourists who came to enjoy the water and picturesque surroundings. The area thus became known as "The Geysers," and the lake and stream thereafter were called Geyser Lake and Geyser Creek.

GEYSER SPRING

Publisher—E. & H.T. Anthony, NYC

This brick building situated on the edge of Coesa Lake served as a small factory in the 1860s, where the owners produced nuts, bolts and iron hardware. It was hardly a place for a tourist to visit. But in 1870, when the owners undertook construction to expand their growing business, a new mineral spring was discovered bubbling from the ground. The owners hired a driller to sink an experimental well, and the Geyser Mineral Spring spouted forth. The nuts and bolts operation ended, and the owners commenced a much more lucrative endeavor. The Geyser became the first of a number of spouting springs discovered in the area. During the rest of the century, untold thousands of visitors ventured to this building and nearby springs, and a visit to the spouters was an important part of the Saratoga experience.

Aetna/Vichy Spring

Photographer—W.H. Baker, Saratoga

In 1872, a wonderful new spring was drilled in the Geysers area and was initially called the Aetna Mineral Spring. (Note the sign above the entrance.) Aetna water was bottled on a limited basis, but its owners had grander visions for the special spring. By 1876, analysis had shown the spring's water was very much like the famed Vichy table water of France. The owners renamed their spouter the Vichy Spring, thus capitalizing on name recognition. The Vichy enjoyed a faithful following, both at the site and in bottles, and throughout the Victorian years it became increasingly popular.

A.E. ALDEN'S PHOTO STUDIO
Photographer—A.E. Alden, Saratoga

Attracting many wealthy travelers, Saratoga was an especially good place for a photographer to set up shop. One of the photographers who came to work the souvenir trade at Saratoga Springs in the 1860s was A.E. Alden of Providence, Rhode Island. Alden established a gallery on Broadway, just south of the entrance to Congress Park, and the elaborate signage out front brought in many customers. Studio portraits were taken here, but a great deal of work was also available by traveling to the tourist sites around Saratoga. In the era of wet plate cameras, photographers frequently had special vans outfitted to carry all the equipment needed to take photos on site. Note on the back of Alden's van the names of other cities where he conducted business. In his absence, local operator/employees carried on his trade at these locations.

TOLL HOUSE/PHOTO WAGON
Photographer—A.E. Alden, Saratoga

Where the tourists went, so did the photographer. Alden stopped by the toll house at Saratoga Lake and captured this scene in the late 1860s. He surely hoped to entice locals to purchase pictures, as well as the wandering tourists. This scene shows the house located on the south side of the lake's Fish Creek outlet. The toll bridge was owned, operated and maintained by a private stock company. In the distance, the road climbing the hill leads back to Saratoga Springs.

BRIGGS HOUSE

Photographer—Wm. Sipperly, Mechanicville, NY

Two carriages are parked out in front of the Briggs House on Saratoga Lake in this 1875/76 photo, labeled "departure of Cornells." Cornell undoubtedly refers to the collegiate team in town for one of the regattas on the lake, events which drew thousands of excited fans. The Briggs was an important staging point for lake country travelers, and a fine table was always set for those seeking a meal.

SARATOGA LAKE

Photographer—Wm. H. Sipperly, Mechanicville, NY

Saratoga Lake was a favorite destination for large numbers of 19th-century visitors. Many came by coach to Moon's Lake House and boat landing, pictured here. From the landing, a tour of the lake was readily secured upon a small steam-powered vessel or sail boat. Fishing on the lake was a popular pastime, as was visiting the many hotels and restaurants on the lake. Snake Hill stands out prominently on the southern side of the lake.

CHAPTER 3
ON THE EVE OF THE OPULENT ERA
Saratoga in the 1860s

As the 1860s began, Saratoga Springs could proudly claim many fine hotels, residences, businesses and spring companies. Brisk growth and expansion had occurred over the 80 years since early settlers carved a community out of the primitive forest. The Victorian era had already long since commenced, and scattered about the town were its influences. Victorian Gothic Revival and Italian Villa buildings were beginning to take the place of structures of an earlier style. But with the High Victorian era at hand, the village's architecture still largely reflected an earlier time when Federal and Greek Revival were in style throughout the country. Saratoga, wonderful as it was, looked much like other prosperous communities in New York and New England. Wood and stone had been the building materials of necessity earlier in the century, but by 1860 brick was often preferred for new commercial and residential construction. Village architecture changed dramatically during the following years, with many buildings of that earlier time passing into memory.

Despite the growing summer crowds, the commercial center of the village had actually grown little during the 19th century. It remained much as it had long been—essentially just a small village. Saratogians knew their season was short and there was no need to significantly expand the central business district, though residential construction would continually push the limits of the village outward. Business owners sought to concentrate everything within a few minutes' walk of the middle of the village, and it was one of the more unique and appreciated features of Saratoga that almost everything was readily at hand for the visitor. As a result, business expansion often came at the expense of small, older structures. They were either torn down or incorporated by some new, larger structure. As some businesses prospered, others were doomed to fail. Opportunities were plentiful, and construction projects were always in the works. In a town not so inclined to such rapid growth, more older build-

ings would likely have remained. Still, with each step along the way, a bit of Saratoga's architectural history survived.

Destructive fires were another, very significant factor which shaped Saratoga during the 19th century. Fires fed insatiably upon the old wood frame and clapboard buildings so prevalent throughout the village. Huge conflagrations swept away in a few hours what had been the work of decades. In the 1860s, there were no hydrants in place to provide a ready water supply for fighting the blazes, and there were no village ordinances requiring fire-resistant construction. Fire fighting, though heroic, was limited by the equipment and methods of the day—hand and steam pumpers and bucket brigades. Often, just saving buildings not yet on fire was all that could be done.

Of the many devastating infernos during the 1860s, the most noteworthy and tragic were the loss of the original United States Hotel in 1865, and Congress Hall in 1866, both of which had been Saratoga landmarks. Yet each tragic fire seemed to spawn excited visions of growth, giving rise to new, grander modern buildings, buildings new in architectural form and adornment. An admirable resiliency of character and outlook always seemed to prevail within the community.

The 1860s and 1870s brought unparalleled destruction, growth and expansion to Saratoga Springs. During these years, the village adapted to many sudden and overwhelming changes, and numerous buildings and businesses vanished into memory. A new era had commenced, and Saratoga would participate in a way quite unlike any village its size in America. The post-Civil War era would bring the new fashion of High Victorian adornment—excessive and stifling to some, but vibrant and inspiring to others.

What did the village look like before the High Victorian era began? What hotels, springs, and businesses greeted the village guests?

OLD FRONT, UNION HALL
Photographer—unknown

Among all the early buildings in Saratoga, Union Hall probably ranked as the best known. This view, published shortly after the Civil War, depicts Union Hall much as it looked during the turbulent war years. On this site, Gideon Putnam erected Saratoga's first hotel and, with increased patronage, Putnam's successors continually enlarged the facility and renamed it Union Hall. Among the many additions was the towering five-story brick structure shown here, built in 1860 on Congress Street. The Union's importance in the village was borne out by the many notable guests and events held here. The old Union operated as a temperance hotel; not allowing the consumption of spirits on the grounds or in the hall was especially popular among the clergy, religious families and the elderly. The temperance movement was active in Saratoga, but parties and entertainment—all proper, of course—were nonetheless plentiful at this old favorite. As ownership and architectural styles changed, and the need to compete for tourists increased, this handsome early structure was gradually transformed into something more grand and suitable to Victorian tastes. Along the way, old furniture and fixtures were deemed antiquated and were replaced, as were the social practices of a bygone era.

UNION HALL PIAZZA
Photographer—unknown

This photo was taken around the time Warren Leland purchased the Union in 1864. Travelers from across a divided nation pass time on the piazza of Union Hall, and may well be caught here discussing the important news of the day, perhaps some recent battle in the great conflict. The wealthy often avoided the horror of war; they had the money and connections to continue making their seasonal visits to Saratoga, where they could safely follow the action in print. Leland, along with his brother, managed the hotel in the post-Civil War years and were continually expanding the establishment. By the summer of 1865, their Union had 737 guest rooms, including 200 which they had added. Under the brothers' ownership, Union Hall became known as Union Hotel, but hard times befell the Lelands, and in 1872 they would lose their Union to one of the richest men in America.

CHESS GAME, UNION HALL
Photographer—unknown

Two elderly gentlemen contemplate their next move in this very early photo, circa 1860, of a chess game held in the "park of Union Hall." Everything about this small group speaks of their wealth and proper upbringing, traits shared with many other seasonal visitors to the Springs. The chess board rests on a cherry one-drawer stand, a popular piece of furniture in the 1820-1850 period, and a holdover from the earlier days at the Union. In the 1870s, when this hotel became the Grand Union Hotel, the cherry, maple and pine furniture of a by-gone period was cast aside, as walnut and marbletop Renaissance Revival, and then later, Eastlake furniture, took its place.

GROUP OF GENTLEMEN, REAR COURTYARD OF UNION HALL

Photographer—unknown

Tourist guidebooks and newspaper accounts usually suggest that Victorian Saratoga was the domain of festive parties, pleasurable pursuits and leisure activities, attended by handsome men and lovely young women. But this photograph paints a different picture, as the sober group of gentlemen at the Union appear neither fun-loving nor ready for much activity at all.

BROADWAY HALL,

W. J. RIGGS.   Saratoga Springs, N. Y.

HALL'S BAND, UNION PARK

Photographer—A.E. Alden, Saratoga

Each day of the season, music filled the air in the park-like grounds laid out behind Union Hotel. In this late-1860s scene, the Lelands have provided pleasant musical entertainment performed by a small brass group, called Hall's Band.

SEVENTH REGIMENT, FRONT OF UNION HOTEL

Photographer—D. Barnum, Boston and Saratoga

In July, 1869, the celebrated Seventh Regiment from New York City gathered at the Springs to hold a reunion. Troops of the well-known Civil War unit are lined up, and the band plays as they stand in formation in front of Union Hotel, the official headquarters of their stay. Many citizens came out to see the Seventh march to patriotic tunes along Broadway. Members of the Seventh enjoyed festivities throughout the village, especially the hops and parties where they danced and flirted with gaily-dressed young women. People across the entire nation learned of the merriment through newspaper accounts and artist renderings appearing in the national press. Saratogians would long remember all the fun of that summer. Other distinguished Civil War veterans visited Saratoga that year, including General Philip Sheridan, a native of nearby Albany who took time out from his military duties out west. Late in the summer season, President Ulysses S. Grant was treated to an especially festive and gracious visit, something he did not always enjoy elsewhere during his troubled presidency. Throughout the remainder of the nineteenth century, Civil War veterans often chose Saratoga as their site to gather and renew old friendships.

OLD UNITED STATES HOTEL

Photographer—D. Barnum, Boston and Saratoga

The old United States Hotel stands at the corner of Broadway and Division Street in this early 1860s view. Its presence here in the village commenced from much more meager beginnings, when it began to welcome summer travelers in 1824 under Elias Benedict and John Ford. When constructed, it was Saratoga's largest and most substantial hotel. Almost every year during the next four decades, much of it under the guidance of owner James Marvin, the hotel grew during the off season. At the time this photo was taken, the hotel had over 500 rooms and was a favorite with many travelers. Tragedy struck this stately hotel and nearby buildings on June 18, 1865, however, when an inferno raged in this central section of the village.

VACANT SITE OF OLD UNITED STATES HOTEL

Photographer—P.H. McKernon, Saratoga

The loss of the old United States Hotel proved even more unbearable as the site remained largely vacant from June, 1865, until 1873. Foundation work finally began in '73 on a new, colossal Victorian version of the United States, whose doors would eventually receive visitors in the summer of 1874. This wonderful image shows the pit and foundation stones left after the fire destroyed the old building. A shack, home to some enterprising barber, must have raised eyebrows, sitting as it does on the Broadway front of the prime commercial site. In the background, on the far left, is Saratoga's old train depot with its tall steeple. It was this early station on Division Street that was replaced by the Victorian depot. The Greek Revival building in the center bears the sign "United States Billiard and Bowling Saloon."

STREET SCENE, FROM OLD UNITED STATES HOTEL PROPERTY

Publisher—E. & H.T. Anthony, NYC

Looking south down Broadway, charred elm trees line the sidewalk and struggle to survive in front of the old United States property. This view dates from the summer of 1865, taken perhaps a month after the June fire, and it is from a widely-distributed series of views of Saratoga published by the Anthony firm in New York City. The large sign in the photo advertises entertainment at the "New Opera House." Located on the grounds of the Union Hotel, the opera house was opened on July 4 of the summer of '65 by the Leland brothers. The owners of the Union had a particularly momentous season. Many Civil War officers visited here, and the Lelands were especially pleased when they were able to entice General U. S. Grant to attend the grand dedication.

JAMES WRIGHT TAILORING ESTABLISHMENT
Photographer—unknown Publisher—Wm. Baker, Saratoga

The Broadway building occupied by tailor James Wright borders Division Street in a block known as Marvin Row. Wright came to Saratoga from New York City in 1855 and worked for a tailoring firm operated here at the Row. In 1858, he purchased the business and continued under his own name. Mending and making clothes, and selling broadcloth, hats, suits and the like, Wright carried on an active trade catering to both summer tourists and residents. Marvin Row occupied a narrow strip of land which was the site of Saratoga's first train depot. The so-called "Row" became available for commercial enterprises when a new depot was built along the rail lines a block west of Broadway in 1837. The Climax Saloon, offering spirits and good times, was a popular business located in the basement of the Row in the late 1850s. But the traveler arriving for the summer of 1865 saw not one of the buildings pictured here. Virtually every building disappeared in the great fire of June, 1865, despite help from fire companies called in from Ballston Spa and far-off Troy. To the left is the old United States, and to the far right is the original Marvin House, first opened for business in the summer of 1853.

J. H. WRIGHT STORE
Photographer—unknown Publisher—Wm. Baker, Saratoga

The loss of Wright's store in the June fire did not deter his efforts to carry on business in the summer of 1865. Saratogians were much too enterprising to let a summer of profits escape. For the season, this shack-like structure sprang to life on his narrow piece of property. By the following summer, however, Marvin House hotel was rebuilt next door to the right, and Wright's shack was demolished, along with any signs of the old Marvin Row. Wright took up business down the street and went on to become president of Saratoga Springs in 1870, and then county treasurer in 1875. In 1879, Wright was removed from the treasurer's office amid charges of fiscal improprieties. He left the area for a time, but soon returned to Saratoga and continued his tailoring business into the late 1880s.

CONGRESS SPRING
Photographer—unknown, probably George Stacy, NYC

This early 1860s closeup shows the ever-present crowd at the Congress, Saratoga's most popular spring. Patrons, perhaps a mix of residents and tourists, wear stove-pipe hats and hoop skirts popular during the Civil War era. Four dipper boys, stationed at this spring and probably at the nearby Columbian, stand on the left in front of the group. People were fascinated by photography and knew that when a photographer was taking stereoscopic pictures, copies could likely end up just about anywhere in the world.

DIPPER BOY, CONGRESS SPRING
Photographer—unknown

Local boys, looking forward to each summer season, were eager to work at the village springs. Tips from the patrons were the economic inducement, but surely the young lads enjoyed the close social contact with many tourists. Watching patrons imbibe the water was an unending source of amusement for the dipper boys, and for anyone else at the springs for that matter. A taste of the water was frequently accompanied by facial contortions, groans of displeasure—and many, it was said, just spit it out. Some hated it, while others loved it. In this mid-1860s view, a dipper boy poses proudly at the source of Congress Water. The long pole with basketlike end held drinking glasses, which were dipped and filled with spring water from the tube below.

UNIDENTIFIED YOUNG GIRL
Photographer—unknown

This charming studio portrait is a "salt print" taken in the early 1850s. The young girl's clothes are typical of that early period, and careful inspection of the backdrop also reveals a clue about its origins. From this perspective, the Congress Pavilion should appear on the left, and the Columbian on the right. In the early days of photography, reversing lenses were not always used and, therefore, a scene can actually appear as a mirror image. The photograph's reflection in a mirror will reveal its true image.

HIGH ROCK SPRING

Photographer—S. Beer, NYC

This rather unimpressive brick pavilion sheltered High Rock Spring and greeted visitors in the early 1860s. High Rock was best known as a historic site and a curiosity of nature with its distinctive mineral cone. Through the pavilion's large, arched, iron-barred opening, the cone is just visible. The small group of visitors seen here was probably drawn by the historic lore associated with the prehistoric mineral deposit, and surely they dipped for a glass of the precious water. Above the arched entrance door, a carved marble frieze reads: "High Rock Building—Erected 1858—by Clarke and White." The firm owned High Rock, in addition to the much more popular Congress Spring and Park, at that time. They did little to improve the historic High Rock setting, preferring to keep their much better known asset in the public's eye. Noteworthy in this view is the absence of any other structure in the immediate vicinity of the spring, and its rather unkempt primitive appearance. The high water table in the spring valley often made the ground muddy, as it appears here. This scene changed dramatically just after the Civil War when new owners erected an appealing pavilion and new bottling house on the site.

IODINE SPRING

Photographer—unknown

Travelers who visited High Rock in the late 1850s saw this view of the Iodine Spring just a couple dozen yards away. The Iodine Spring pavilion and bottling house were built in the 1830s, and in the years after the Civil War its popularity and changing styles altered its early, almost primitive-looking character. The spring's discovery goes back to the late 1700s, when it was called the Gunpowder Spring. It soon became known as the President. When analysis by new owners in 1834 showed iodine among the water's many components, it took on the new identity and name pictured here. In the 1860s, its name changed again, to the Star Spring. While many mineral fountains kept their original name over the years, others, like the Iodine, went through frequent changes. Surely this spring holds the distinction for having the most names.

EMPIRE SPRING PROPERTY
Photographer—unknown

The Greek Revival buildings pictured here in spring valley belonged to the owners of the Empire Spring. The structures were erected shortly after 1848, when George W. Weston and Company developed the commercial potential of the spring. This early view looks north, taken from Circular Street as it descends the hill heading into spring valley, and it pre-dates residential development in the area. High Rock and Star Springs are located just to the left, out of view. Note that Willow Walk, the name of High Rock Avenue at the time, ended at the Empire property. A ditch, barely visible, running along the bottom of the hill, drained the ever-present flow of surface water in the valley. Beyond the Empire property on the sloping land are a scattering of old homes and barns. In earlier times, huge lime kilns operated on the slope. Outcroppings along the valley's limestone escarpment, and an abundance of wood fuel for the furnaces, provided the means to turn out this vital product.

CLOSE-UP OF EMPIRE SPRING
Photographers—Beer Brothers, NYC

This wonderful closeup of the Empire Spring pavilion shows patrons draped in garb typical of the Civil War era. Two cast-iron lions proudly stand guard over the medicinal spring and help attest to the water's powerful natural properties. In all likelihood, the decorative lions were placed here by owner George Weston during his development and expansion of the spring in the 1850s. During that period, the water was bottled inside the little building at the left and was Congress Spring's chief competitor. By the mid-1860s, new owners, the Empire Spring Co., and then the Congress and Empire Spring Co., replaced all these older structures with a "modern" brick bottling house and pavilion. The small Greek Revival pavilion shown here was actually saved during the makeover and moved to private property a short distance from the spring. It was enclosed and served as a small residence until June, 1871, when it was destroyed by fire.

C.R. BROWN PROPERTY, BROADWAY
Photographers—Beer Brothers, NYC

Typical of the early style of buildings which welcomed Saratoga visitors in 1860 was this one on Broadway. Located across from Congress Park, it was erected in the early 1830s and used initially as a grocery store. Charles R. Brown purchased the building in 1861 and became a prosperous businessman, conducting an optical and jewelry business. Clocks, silver hollow-ware and fancy goldplate jewelry were among his offerings at the year-round establishment. Brown also operated a boarding house at the site, letting rooms on the second floor to travelers. The small sign over the doorway reads, " Park House of C.R. Brown." The success of Brown's business venture here is especially admirable given his condition when he first arrived in Saratoga. In 1858, in his native Otsego County, Brown suffered a horrible accident which among other complications, left his legs permanently paralyzed. Near death and considered a helpless invalid, he was brought to the Springs the following year, where it was hoped the mineral water and therapy would be of benefit. For two years, Brown boarded at Dr. Bedortha's Water Cure, just to the right of the building seen here. But disaster again challenged Brown on July 4, 1864, when this building and many others were destroyed by fire. After the inferno, the optimistic and energetic Brown purchased Bedortha's property and erected new buildings, called the Park Place Block.

Fire Department. ·

RESIDENCE AND FAMILY
Photographers—Baker and Record, Saratoga

This charming photograph shows a residential scene travelers might encounter if they left the bustling center of the village. The family undoubtedly had the local photography firm capture this image for their family album. Although the photo was taken in the early 1870s, it displays a style of residential architecture typical throughout the country during the 1830-1860 period. Homes of this classic form and straight line construction yielded during the High Victorian period to profuse ornamentation.

PINE GROVE, CHANCELLOR WALWORTH'S HOUSE

Publisher—Hall Brothers, Brooklyn, NY

In 1815, Judge Henry Walton, one of Saratoga's largest property holders, built this fine home on Broadway just west of High Rock Spring. In 1823, Walton sold the house to Reuben Hyde Walworth, who was appointed Chancellor of the State of New York in 1828. While neither magnificent nor palatial, from that time on the unassuming building became one of the best-known residences in Saratoga Springs, visited by some of our nation's most well-known statesmen and artists. Among the callers at the house were DeWitt Clinton, Martin Van Buren, Stephen Douglas, Millard Fillmore, James Buchanan, Washington Irving, James Fenimore Cooper, Joseph Bonaparte and Daniel Webster, to name but a few.

The Chancellor's home and nearby property was known as "Pine Grove." The grounds were often more like a public park than a private homesite. Swings hung among the trees and were said to be always filled. Tenpins and lawn games were popular pastimes here, and the setting proved a pleasant place to picnic. For many summers, Indians camped among the trees and sold their bows, beadwork and trinkets to summer guests. Railroad lines eventually split up the Walworth property and made it less picturesque. An expanding village also meant new development nearby. In 1860, the house was materially altered (roof line and second story mostly) to the form shown in this view; the first floor was left unchanged. In 1867, Walworth passed away, and in the early 1870s the home became a young ladies' school and family hotel. But the classic structure passed into history by 1885, when the family transformed it into a 55-room Queen Anne mansion.

OLD WATER TOWER, CONGRESS SPRING PARK

Publisher—G.O. Brown and Co., Baltimore, MD

This was an early water tower built in Congress Park by Dr. John Clarke. Clarke built the reservoir to collect and store water from fresh water springs nearby. The tower supplied water to Union and Congress Halls, and to a few other buildings by using wooden pipes laid underground. The reservoir became obsolete as the village demand for water grew, and larger, more efficient supplies were needed. The aging tower was finally removed from the setting during the high-Victorian makeover of the park.

CHAPTER 4

MINERAL SPRINGS—SARATOGA'S FOUNDATION

Geography and geology are always crucial factors in the settlement and growth of any community. In the early days of America, towns sprouted up along rivers or in the midst of fertile land. Saratoga's early settlers found a region unremarkable and undistinguishable from the surrounding primitive wilderness, except for one very special feature—the mineral springs upon which the community would build its fortunes.

The special properties of mineral waters have long been appreciated for the healing and comfort they offer. Ancient Greece and Rome, and other civilizations throughout the world, bear evidence to the long-standing universal appeal of these health-giving waters. In the case of Saratoga, native Iroquois had used the spring for countless years before the first white man set foot upon American soil, and it was they who first revealed the High Rock Spring to Europeans.

Mineral springs have long been sought out and consumed by animals as well. During the early days of settlement at High Rock, deer and other game were often seen drinking the water and licking the mineral deposits at the springs. Huge flocks of passenger pigeons (now extinct) were said to occasionally congregate about the cone until encroaching civilization forced them away.

While travelers had braved the wilderness to visit the revered High Rock ever since its "discovery," the rapid growth of the surrounding village in the first half of the 19th century was largely the result of Dr. John Clarke's successful efforts in promoting Congress Spring. It was Clarke who began a great industry by exporting the water. Other highly successful owners of spring water companies followed in his footsteps as more springs were located. Through their efforts and enterprises, Saratoga's mineral water became available throughout the country and to much of the rest of the world. It was the mineral fountains which first drew the attention and crowds, and from which all other businesses evolved.

Unique circumstances are necessary for mineral springs to develop, and Saratoga possessed just the right elements.

There was a consistent pattern to where the bubbling saline fountains were found, with most located in the vicinity of the geologic fault running along the western edge of the shallow valley passing through the middle of the village. Located just east of Broadway, the drainage basin was appropriately known as "spring valley." Early on, many of the springs were discovered by chance, but as time went on others were revealed through scientific study and exploration.

With the growing popularity of the springs, scientists and physicians were soon drawn to the village to study the water. Without exception, they found that nature created each spring with a unique chemical composition. No two were exactly alike, despite some veins of water being tapped only a few yards apart. Analysis deemed some springs unsuitable for commercial development, while others were destined for bottling and bathing. Spring owners often proudly proclaimed the virtues of their water by citing scientific testimonials. In the years before the Civil War, only a few companies actually carried on the very profitable business of selling bottled water outside the region. But from about 1860 on, sales increased dramatically, and new spring companies formed to join in the trade. This new era of rapid expansion could be seen in the much greater numbers of wagons and railroad freight cars departing from Saratoga heavily laden with carefully packed cases of bottles and kegs. Untold numbers went to New York, Boston and other ports to be packed aboard ships for transport overseas, or for consumption en route by affluent passengers. Passengers aboard trains crossing the continent, or upon side-wheelers plying the Mississippi River, would occasionally hear "High Rock", "Congress Water" or "Excelsior" being shouted out en route, and they would purchase a bottle to quench their thirst.

Back in Saratoga, well-attended bathhouses were operated at those springs which were deemed especially good for bathing. Water cures were promoted, and medical facilities opened, offering a variety of waters and health regimens. The treatments were often said to refresh and renew one's vigor, and owners advertised widely to attract patrons. The sick, the desperate and the healthy came from afar, anxious to improve their condition. Some baths offered little more than submersion in a tub, while others were sophisticated facilities open for both walk-ins and long-term boarders. These establishments made Saratoga much more than just a watering place: they helped create its reputation as a health spa.

A very significant new chapter in the history of Saratoga's fortunes began in the 1870s when an area about one and one-half miles south of the village was found to hold wonderful sources of water far beneath the earth's surface. Wells were drilled and the bubbling water spouted forth under the pressure of trapped carbonic acid gas. The spouters, as these springs were called, were awe-inspiring curiosities and attracted huge numbers of visitors to the area of Saratoga which became known as Geyserville, or simply, "The Geysers." Some spouters were said to be so highly charged with gas that they seemed to flow like foam from a soda fountain. Attractive spring houses and park-like grounds were built, water from the spouters was bottled, and a new and lucrative component was added to Saratoga's economy.

Along with the obvious economic benefits derived from affluent guests gathering each summer, there were also many spin-off activities which directly supported the water business and provided employment to local residents year round. Coopers produced barrels and kegs for mineral water, while teamsters busily ferried the supplies and products. Local builders were employed to erect bottling houses and pavilions, while well drillers and laborers were kept busy searching the earth for more water. Young children earned pocket change serving water at the spring pavilions each summer, and still others carried water to the village hotels to be served to guests.

Noteworthy among the ancillary enterprises was the manufacture of glass bottles. Most bottles were initially purchased from a glass factory in central New York operated by Oscar Granger and company. But in the mid-1840s, Granger moved the glass factory to Mount Pleasant, near Lake Desolation in Saratoga County, where, for a period of 20 years, the company continued operation. In 1866, Granger's glassworks was purchased by the Congress and Empire Spring Company, which moved the factory to a new site just south of the village. Most, but not all, of the local spring water companies had their bottles manufactured there. During the cool weather of the slow seasons, the furnaces were fired up and workers produced millions of bottles. The operation was described in a newspaper account in February, 1876, when the factory was busy producing an order for Geyser Spring. That one order alone was for 1000 gross of pints and 200 gross of quarts—a staggering total of 172,800 bottles. The new Saratoga site was called Congressville. The fascinating art of glassblowing drew inquisitive visitors who found the operation an interesting and informative way to pass time.

Just what was so special about this water? What was it good for? What should the visitor expect when arriving at Saratoga?

Saratoga Springs, as a popular resort, has steadily grown from year to year; and its magnificent prosperity must have some substantial and enduring foundation, or it would have faded into obscurity long since, before the unreasoning caprice of fashion. Its springs are the secret of its success. Its mineral waters flow in exhaustless abundance from year to year, and, though given away freely to all who care to ask for them, and, in bottles or barrels, sent to every state, and half over Europe, they run to waste in countless thousands of gallons. Upon these free flowing rivers, bubbling from the hillside, or spouting in snow white fountains half a hundred feet into the air, Saratoga has built her faith and her hotels, and has not been disappointed. While the waters flow, Saratoga will flourish and bloom in all the glory of splendid palaces. Added to these are the natural beauties of the place, and the quite as pleasing results that have sprung from the mingled art and nature. ... Geological and scientific people have spent much time in seeking to explain the origin or source of these waters. Rain water is the usual source of spring-waters. It soaks down through porous soils and rocks ... on its way it absorbs saline and other mineral substances and gases, and, loaded with them, it reaches the surface, charged in varying proportions, and having a fixed character as mineral water. The proportions do not change materially; and from year to year the waters flow unchanged, and produce on all who drink of them the same general effects. ... The carbonic acid gas held in the water doubtless aids it in finding an outlet to the surface. Being con-

fined under pressure, it seeks to escape, and brings the water with it. ... The first taste of the water is not always lovely. After the first blush, the water becomes exceedingly enjoyable and one is tempted to indulge too freely in the pungent, acidulous and salty mixture. The after-effects resemble those of soda-water, and, if a large quantity is taken, there follows a sense of fullness, perhaps a slight giddiness in the head and a desire for sleep. These symptoms are only slight, and are soon removed by the discharges that follow; and afterwards there comes increased appetite and a feeling of comfortable serenity that is very satisfactory. ... The commercial value of the springs is a fair measure of their medicinal value. Property in mineral springs is costly. They are difficult to manage, they demand many thousands to properly tube them and a good bottling plant involves a large outlay. ... Most of the springs are owned and managed by joint-stock companies, with a capital varying from a hundred thousand dollars to a million or more. ... the only profit that results from the springs is found in the sale of the water, in bottles and barrels, in distant places. At Saratoga Springs one may drink all one pleases, and carry it away by the pailful for the asking, or an optional fee to the dipper-boy. The outlook for the spring-water business is said to be good in spite of the disasters that have overtaken some of the spring companies. The demand for pure natural mineral waters is steadily increasing. People are beginning to know the difference between the villainous compounds mixed in city cellars with marble dust, gas, and seawater salts and the pure, limpid, and pearly waters that here spring up to the sunlight from Nature's great laboratory. There is sort of free fight going on between the chemical waters and the spring waters, and sensible people are rapidly learning which side to take, and are becoming more cautious which they drink. There is no need to be deceived, even in distant cities, as the protected trade marks on corks of all bottles show the real spring waters whatever kind, and this, with the marks on the boxes and bottles, ought to make one safe in buying a half dozen, even if one lives in England, Australia or California. Another curious feature in this connection is the fact that no mixture, however skillfully put together, can exactly imitate the natural waters, nor can any mineral water from the chemists ever produce so good results as the same quantity of true springwater. This is one reason why people flock to Saratoga in such vast crowds. They

wish to select for themselves, and to use their own particular goblets, and to know certainly whereof they drink. ... Perhaps there is no class of mineral water drinkers who enjoy a visit to Saratoga so much, or who realize so fully and so speedily the benefits arising from drinking the water, as the class of persons known as "free livers." They suffer from functional disturbance arising from too much food. But when daily drinking the water they are wholly exempt from all inconvenience arising from such surfeit not only, but can use double the quantity of food and drinks previously taken, and experience no inconvenience. ... The diseases affected by the waters are numerous. To give a list in detail would be useless and confusing, and perhaps harmful. There is but one course to pursue in drinking the spring waters for the health's sake. Consult a resident physician, let him make a diagnosis of your case, and, under his advice, select the particular spring of most value to you, and govern yourself, in all things, by his experiences and acquaintances with the waters. The medical staff of Saratoga is excellent, and one may rely on their ability to assist and direct. ... Above all, do not be led away by the gratuitous advice of persons who have been benefited by these waters, but who are not possessed of sufficient medical knowledge to give a reason for their belief in any particular spring. Concerning the directions for their use, much the same thing may be said. Each user of these healing waters must in measure be a law unto himself. To drink any and all of the waters would be simply unreasonable. Seek proper advice, and then follow it, and be not led aside by the enthusiasm of some invalid who thinks it a cure for all diseases. ... To persons in perfectly good health the waters do no particular harm, even if indulged in freely. At the same time, there is reason in all things, and if one is really unwell, there is but one thing to do—consult a medical man."[4]

CONGRESS AND COLUMBIAN SPRINGS
Publisher—G.O. Brown and Co., Baltimore, MD

Undoubtedly this was the most important and best-known spring site in 19th-century America. This circa-1870 scene shows Congress Spring pavilion on the right, and the Columbian beyond on the left. For many summer visitors, a morning trip to these springs was an important part of the Saratoga experience. Fond memories of the park, and a belief in the medicinal effects of the bubbling saline water, induced many of these same visitors to purchase bottles of mineral water throughout the year.

COLUMBIAN SPRING
Photographer—Charles Bierstadt, Niagara Falls, NY

Located only a few yards from the Congress, the Columbian was discovered by Gideon Putnam in 1803 as he cleared land. The Columbian, with its strong iron taste, never enjoyed the widespread popularity and acclaim of its neighbor. And unlike its neighbor, Columbian Spring water wasn't available in bottles for many years, until after the Civil War, when the owner at the time, the Congress and Empire Spring Company, sold the water in pint and quart quantities.

WASHINGTON SPRING
Photographer—Wm. H. Sipperly,
Mechanicville, NY

Located along Broadway in the well-kept gardens adjacent to the Clarendon Hotel, Washington Spring was another early mineral spring tubed by Gideon Putnam. Throughout the first half of the nineteenth century, it was used primarily as a bathing spring, the patrons believing it cured various skin ailments. The spring, and the grounds to the right of the photo, were part of a recreation park in the 1840s and 50s; along with a mineral bath-house, there were a bowling alley, shooting gallery, and billiards room. A small pond found here was used by children to sail toy boats and by preachers to baptize believers. Like many of Saratoga's mineral springs, the Washington changed ownership over the years, each new owner having some grand vision to better promote and market the waters. By the 1860s, the remains of the recreation park were gone. The Washington was then being promoted by its owner, John White, who distributed the water in bottles. In 1873, Charles Leland purchased the Washington and incorporated it into the Clarendon Hotel property he had purchased earlier.

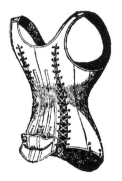

CROWD AT WASHINGTON SPRING
Photographer—unknown

The pavilion over the Washington Spring was quite unlike any other in Saratoga, many likening the picturesque tiny cover to a witch's peaked hat. This very colorful scene was captured in August, 1867, with the two young women in the front surely making the most fashionable statement among the assemblage.

HATHORN SPRING

Photographers—Baker and Record, Saratoga

A fire in August, 1868, destroyed the barns of the Exchange Hotel and several other buildings located on Spring Street across from a newly-rebuilt Congress Hall. Henry Hathorn, owner of the Congress Hall, saw opportunity when, after the fire, he looked at the vacant pit and judged it to be a good location for a ballroom, something lacking in his new hotel. Hathorn purchased the property, and during excavation for his new building, a stone mason discovered mineral water trickling from the ground. Hathorn was especially pleased by the find, although the discovery of another mineral spring in the area caused considerable concern for the nearby Congress and Empire Spring Company. In this view, from about 1875, the fruits of Hathorn's efforts are clearly evident. Hathorn's ballroom was located in the building behind the spring. By the 1880s, a commodious enclosed drink hall was built behind the ballroom to shelter the spring. Inside, Hathorn Water was bottled and served at a wonderful fountainhead in a decorative setting that encouraged patrons to relax and enjoy the water. They were also enticed to purchase Saratoga souvenirs and other fancy tourist goods in a section known as Myer's Oriental Bazaar. The fears of the Congress and Empire Spring Company proved to be correct, as Hathorn Spring water was soon highly regarded, and, by the 1890s, the Hathorn boasted sales of bottled water which exceeded those of all other Saratoga springs combined.

Myers' Oriental Bazaar.

CRYSTAL SPRING AND PARK PLACE HOTEL
Photographer—Unknown

In 1869, Charles R. Brown, a Broadway merchant and hotel owner, launched plans to drill a new well on property formerly occupied by A.E. Alden's Photograph Gallery, just across from the Columbian and Congress Springs. The effort produced the Crystal Spring in 1870. Brown next expanded his holdings with the five-story mansard edifice pictured here. Known as the new Park Place Hotel, the building was described in an 1871 gazetteer advertisement as follows: "contains on the second floor a spacious, open, Arcade Promenade Gallery, and on the first floor immediately below rises within an elegant colonnade, the limpid health giving waters of the Crystal Spring, accessible from the hotel."[5] Much to his dismay, Brown watched all his efforts go up in smoke as this new building came to an end in a huge fire in October, 1871. Undeterred, Brown bought additional property and, along with Dr. Hamilton of the old Crescent Hotel and medical institute, erected the mammoth Grand Central Hotel. The Crystal Spring was again given prominence in the hotel setting and was dispensed to the public from a street-level fountain counter on the front of the Grand Central.

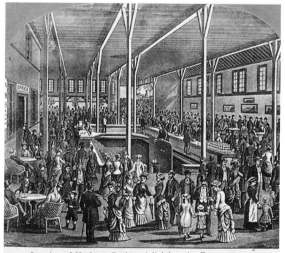

Interior of Hathorn Spring---Adjoining the Bazaar.

CRYSTAL SPRING

Photographer—Unknown

This fine little pavilion, erected in 1875, was the third public fountain created for Crystal Spring in just five years. It was put up after another fire in late 1874 destroyed the colossal Grand Central Hotel built by Brown and Hamilton. Crystal Spring Water Company continued to bottle and sell the Crystal's water after the 1874 fire, but this, too, would cease within a few years. Despite ongoing efforts to promote the Crystal, it never was very widely received in the marketplace, probably due to the fact that neither astute businessmen like Brown and his successors nor a pleasant sounding name like Crystal could hide the fact that it smelled awful. Behind the spring is the front porch of the new Columbian Hotel, erected in 1872 after a fire in October, 1871.

HAMILTON SPRING

Photographer—unknown

As the sign on this charming pavilion advertises, the Hamilton Spring was used primarily for bathing. The Hamilton was discovered by Gideon Putnam, who erected the first bathhouse at the site. This classic Greek pavilion was built in the late 1830s while Dr. John Clarke owned the property. The Hamilton was located behind Congress Hall at the corner of Spring and Putnam Streets, which, in the nineteenth century, extended to Congress Street. The baths were located just behind the small pavilion.

Beyond the structure, to the left, was Garrison's Livery and Boarding stable, whose sign is visible on Spring Street.

The stereocard from which this view is taken has an interesting history itself. A label affixed to the back indicates it is card number 844 from the Stereoscopic Collection of Mrs. Hanson E. Weaver. Weaver, who lived in Gettysburg, Pennsylvania, was a pioneer collector of stereoviews, amassing a large and varied collection in the 1860s and 70s. Having the foresight to recognize the important historical nature of the cards, she placed a small identifying label on each. Long after Weaver passed away and the collection was dispersed, collectors still eagerly seek out her views.

HAMILTON SPRING, VICTORIAN PAVILION
Photographers—Baker and Record, Saratoga

Shortly after the so-called Exchange Hotel fire in August, 1868 consumed many buildings in this area, the Hamilton was rebuilt and given a pavilion somewhat similar to its original. But in 1879, the pavilion was materially altered to the form seen in this photograph. During that decade, the spring was popular primarily with the "locals." No longer operated with a bath-house, the water was consumed on site and bottled on a very limited basis. The building behind the spring is a dwelling erected in the early 1870s.

UNITED STATES AND PAVILION SPRINGS
Photographers—McDonnald and Sterry, Albany and Saratoga

This decorative Victorian structure, built in 1869, covers the United States and Pavilion Springs. Although located right next to each other, each spring's chemical makeup and curative properties were markedly different. Located just off Pavilion Place between Lake Avenue and Caroline street, each enjoyed a following at the spring and in bottles.

The Pavilion Spring was first tubed during the winter of 1839/40. At that time, the site was nothing but swamp. When the ground was frozen, Daniel McLaren, owner of the nearby Pavilion Hotel, began excavating it in search of a mineral spring. A fine source was discovered and McLaren called it the Pavilion Spring. Much to the dismay of local citizens, McLaren decided to charge patrons for taking water at the spring site. This was not in keeping with a long-standing Saratoga tradition.

A revolt ensued, and a boycott of the spring was planned. During the following summer, a huge crowd of local leaders, citizens and summer guests met near Congress Park to plan their strategy. Once he learned just how strongly the public felt, McLaren relented and his water, like that of other springs in the village, was given free of charge at the site.

SELTZER AND HIGH ROCK SPRINGS
Photographer—Wm. H. Sipperly,
Mechanicville, NY

Patrons sample water at the Seltzer Spring on the left, and the High Rock beyond, in this scene from the early 1870s. The Seltzer Spring, believed to be the only true seltzer water ever discovered in the United States, was not developed commercially until the late 1860s, when the spring's source was located and tubed by its owner, Dr. Haskins. Earlier in the nineteenth century, it had been known as the Barrel Spring because the mineral water was collected in a wooden barrel placed in the swampy ground surrounding the spring. The brick bottling house shown here was erected after 1868; the projecting open section in front served an eager public. When the new High Rock pavilion and bottling house, and then the Seltzer were built, the land in this area was filled in and raised to eliminate much of the swampiness found there.

SELTZER SPRING COMPANY
Publisher—E. & H.T. Anthony, NYC

This closeup shows the front of the Seltzer with a young dipper boy poking his head out from behind the column and counter. Just behind the boy, on the floor of the serving area, the owners contrived an interesting glass container to secure the water as it flowed out of the ground. This allowed patrons to view the bubbling of the mineral water. By the 1880s, this building also housed the Natural History Museum of Dr. Haskins. Visitors could view what was advertised as one of the country's most extensive private collections of specimens of fauna, geology, mineralogy, paleontology and archeology.

DIPPER BOY, HIGH ROCK SPRING

Photographers—Baker and Record, Saratoga

Compared to other dipper boys seen in period photographs, this lad appears younger than most. Visiting patrons had their glasses lowered into the cone and filled, and many gave a small payment to the boy.

HIGH ROCK SPRING

Photographer—Charles Bierstadt, Niagara Falls, NY

A gilded carved eagle sits atop the picturesque High Rock Spring pavilion, completed in 1866, a product of Seymour Ainsworth and William McCaffrey. Other springs in the city would surpass the High Rock in commercial popularity, but it was always a revered and honored location. Behind the pavilion, owners built a bottling house to prepare water for the marketplace. When the partners initiated the project to commercialize the spring, they actually removed the conelike mineral deposit and set it aside while they dug the ground to secure the spring's source. In anticipation of this project, many Saratogians expressed concern that the historic cone would be damaged or destroyed. As it turned out, the job was easily accomplished as the base of deposit was located only a few inches below the ground. Interestingly, the excavation was much like an archeological dig. It was said that workmen found evidence of early trees and ancient campfires deep below the cone. When the project was finally completed, few recognized that the location of the cone was slightly moved from where it had been for centuries. In this view, the picket fence beyond High Rock separates the Star Spring property. Note the small shack with the slanted roof behind the fence on the left. This small building, a privy/outhouse, was a necessary convenience before indoor plumbing, public sewer lines and health codes rendered them obsolete.

CHARLES MCNUTT

Photographer—P.H. McKernon, Saratoga

Charles McNutt is listed in an 1871 county directory as a sawyer and farmer who worked 50 acres near Middle Grove. One day in the mid-1860s, he put on this dashing suit, visited Saratoga and had his picture taken.

BIRDSEYE VIEW OF HIGH ROCK SPRING

Photographers—Kilburn Brothers, Littleton, NH

An enterprising photographer produced this interesting view when he took this photo from atop the Star Spring bottling house about 1870. Looking south, a path leads from the Star Spring property to High Rock; just beyond is the Seltzer Spring. Both bottling houses are built with their backs to the escarpment, which forms the western side of the spring valley. Far off in the distance, the towers of Congress Hall are visible.

STAR SPRING

Photographer—unknown

Owners of the Star Spring in the 1860s placed a picket fence around the property and gave the public access through an arched gate. The mineral water of this spring was well known throughout the country, with large kegs sold to grocers, druggists and soda fountain operators.

CLOSE-UP OF STAR SPRING

Photographer—unknown

This wonderful mid-1860s photo shows a close view of the entrance to Star Spring. It was also referred to simply as "The Saratoga Spring," as the sign indicates. A few patrons, some children—possibly working around the spring for pocket change—and dipper boys pose for this charming picture.

STAR SPRING

Photographers—Baker and Record, Saratoga

The Star prospered and, to handle the increased business, the small wood-frame bottling house was replaced by this large, brick Victorian building. The owners kept their classic pavilion over the Star and did not "Victorianize" it, as did many spring owners in the village during that era.

EMPIRE SPRING

Photographer—unknown

This spring pavilion and bottling house welcomed a whole new generation of post-war Saratoga travelers. These buildings were erected when Chauncy Kilmer and his Empire Spring Company owned the popular spring, replacing the out-dated Greek Revival buildings of an earlier era. The cast-iron lions were all that remained from the old days when George Weston operated the bottling operation here in the 1850s.

EMPIRE SPRING

Photographer—unknown

A pleasing glimpse of the Empire Spring pavilion is given by this closeup. The grounds were tastefully laid out with greenery and decorative cast-iron urns, and benches added to the pleasant scene. Beyond the spring to the left, Circular Street climbs the small hill along the eastern side of spring valley.

OLD RED SPRING

Photographer—Saratoga Photograph Co., Saratoga

Visitors had been making their way to the Old Red Spring for a hundred years by the time this photograph was taken in the 1870s. The Old Red was located a short distance northeast of the High Rock and Empire springs, on what was then called Spring Avenue. Primarily used for medicinal bathing, it was said to cure, among other conditions, a variety of skin problems. While re-excavating the Old Red in 1871 for a new bathhouse, another vein of mineral water was found and given the name Red Spring. The "new" Red enjoyed a good trade in bottled form. The large clientele of this bathhouse is attested by its guest journal/register. On August 20, 1876, for example, at least 45 patrons signed in to bathe. They left comments in the register ranging from "delightful" to "the water taste too flat." The journal also reveals that on both September 20 and 23, 1876, well- known Saratoga gambler, politician and track promoter John Morrissey signed in for a bath. It provides an interesting chronicle of the far-off places Saratoga visitors came from during that summer of 1876: Dakota Territory, London, Chicago, Savannah, Havana, Baltimore, Brazil, Mexico, Paris, Richmond, Providence, Brooklyn, Texas. Of course, many others traveled from places closer by, such as Albany, Troy, Cohoes, Cambridge, Whitehall and Glens Falls.[6]

EXCELSIOR SPRING
Photographer—D. Barnum, Boston and Saratoga

The Excelsior Spring was the best-known of the mineral waters found in the area of Saratoga known as the Valley of the Ten Springs. Commercially developed by the Lawrence family, this spring and the adjacent area was a popular excursion for guests from the big hotels who wanted to escape the bustling activity of the village's center. The Valley of the Ten Springs derived its name from the fact that numerous springs were found near here when the area was first being explored late in the eighteenth century. This lovely scene by Deloss Barnum is from a series of photographs taken of tourists visiting the site one summer afternoon in 1869.

EXCELSIOR SPRING AND CARRIAGE
Photographer—D. Barnum, Boston and Saratoga

A horse-drawn coach stands in wait while its passengers drink at Excelsior Spring. Painted on the coach are colorful vignettes, decorative panels and pinstriped lines; across the top of the open passenger compartment, the name of the spring is boldly painted. It is not known if this coach was operated by the spring company, or if it was independently run; surely, however, it worked the route from the hotels and the village center to the Excelsior. This charming photo is from the same Barnum series as the previous view.

EXCELSIOR SPRING, VICTORIAN BOTTLING HOUSE

Photographers—Baker and Record, Saratoga

Like other prosperous mineral water companies, the owners of the Excelsior expanded their facilities as business demanded. Bolstered by an increase in sales, a handsome Victorian brick edifice became the company's new bottling house in the 1870s. When building the new facility, the owners developed a unique apparatus to insure carbonation was not lost in the bottle and keg operation. Excelsior water was very popular in soda fountains and drug stores throughout the country. It was always as fresh and pure as it could be, thanks to the Lawrence invention. Locally, Excelsior was often dispensed from fountains set up in the hotels for their guests. A few yards behind and to the right of the bottling house, the Lawrence family also operated the Union Spring. It, too, was bottled, but never enjoyed the popularity of the Excelsior.

EUREKA SPRING

Photographers—Baker and Record, Saratoga

Traveling further from the village along the Valley of the Ten Springs, visitors next encountered the Eureka Spring, pictured here, and White Sulphur Spring, located close by. The Eureka was discovered in 1866. A couple of years later, the new owner, A.R. Dyett, a New York City attorney, had the land cleared to create a picturesque park, and he began to bottle the water. Despite being a lesser-known Saratoga spring, sale of bottled Eureka still supported extensive distribution from Saratoga and New York City offices.

WHITE SULPHUR SPRING

Photographer—D. Barnum, Boston and Saratoga

This circa-1870 view shows the White Sulphur Spring bathhouse and bottling plant, located only a few yards from Eureka Spring. The healing waters of this large bathhouse made it a prosperous and well-attended operation. Water from the Eureka was also bottled in this building, since Dyett owned both springs. This spring should not be confused with another spring located on Saratoga Lake which was also called White Sulphur Spring.

VICHY SPRING AND GEYSER LAKE

Photographers—Baker and Record, Saratoga

This peaceful scene on Geyser Lake shows the small facility built over the Vichy Spring not long after its discovery in 1872, when it was called Aetna Spring. Located near Cady Hill, south of the village, the popular spring had a large following. Increased business in the 1880s necessitated expansion of the bottling house, and it gained international recognition. It is hard to imagine this picturesque little facility and its renowned water raising the ire of a foreign government, but French officials, upset over the supposed infringement of "their" Vichy, would one day sue the company in an attempt to discontinue its use of the name.

INTERIOR VICHY SPRING

Photographers—Baker and Record, Saratoga

A lovely cast-iron fountain was located just inside the Vichy pavilion. In this scene, affluent-appearing visitors draw mineral water from a spigot at the side of the decorative fountain.

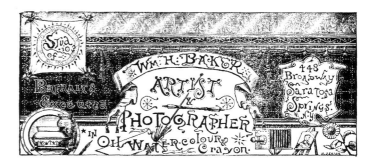

INTERIOR GEYSER SPRING

Photographer—Wm. Sipperly, Mechanicville, NY

A handsome crowd at the counter poses for the photographer in this mid-1870s interior scene at Geyser Spring. A large bottling operation was carried on here, and many tourists came to see the area and sample the famed springwater. The company boasted in its advertising that, in 1871, 150,000 visitors enjoyed the site and that in 1872, as its popularity increased, a quarter million people visited. While in the vicinity, guests could stroll in the lovely park laid out around the facility and purchase souvenirs, including stereoviews of all the popular Saratoga spots, at a small gift shop. Only a short walk away, the Champion Spouting and the Vichy were other popular tourist destinations. Note the hole cut in the ceiling to allow the spring freedom to spout. The clear glass globe-like apparatus in the center allowed viewing of the bubbling action of the highly carbonated waters.

GLACIER SPOUTING SPRING/CHAMPION SPOUTING

Publishers—Hall Brothers, Brooklyn, NY

In the fall of 1871, a local well driller was hired to sink a shaft near Geyser Spring in hopes that another mineral water fountain might be found. The effort produced Saratoga's most magnificent spouter. When first developed, it was called the Glacier Spouting Spring, but shortly after the name was changed to Champion Spouting. Here the flow is shown restricted by a pipe with a small nozzle on the end of it. The Champion became a favorite tourist attraction. During the summer months, large crowds gathered at five o'clock in the afternoon. The spring was uncapped and a foaming jet of water spouted to a height of over 100 feet.

CHAMPION SPOUTING SPRING, WINTER
Photographers—Baker and Record, Saratoga

This winter scene depicts the ice cone which formed around the Champion Spouting Spring as water spouted forth and then froze. Winters provided the various spring companies in Saratoga an opportunity to put all their efforts into bottling water, as few tourists came beyond the summer season.

If not delivered in Ten Days return to

ALEX. McQUEEN,

Schuyler, Saratoga Co., N. Y.

TRITON SPOUTING SPRING
Photographers—Baker and Record, Saratoga

This little wood-frame building was home to Triton Spouting Spring, located on Geyser Lake across from the Vichy. Two decorative cast-iron figures stand in front of the building to welcome visitors. At the center of the roof ridge was an opening which the owners could use to let the spring spout freely.

TRITON SPRING HOUSE, INTERIOR
Photographer—unknown

Mineral water bottles and mugs line the counter in this rare circa-1875 interior photo of the Triton Spring house. All the bottles are embossed with the Triton name, as is the barrel on the floor. Barely visible in the middle, appearing as a light white line, is the Triton stream spouting from the ground below the counter. Interestingly, the photographer placed a black cloth on the back wall so that the springwater might more easily be seen in the photo. Certainly, pride of ownership and bit of showmanship has been employed in staging this photo.

CHAPTER 5

CONGRESS SPRING AND PARK

Congress Park and its namesake mineral water fountain have long been considered one of Saratoga's crown jewels. Located in the center of the village, the picturesque setting, made pleasant by the handiwork and care of man and nature, was an important social venue and rural escape for residents and tourists alike. No trip to Saratoga was complete without a stroll through the park and a glass of its highly-acclaimed water.

The land around the Congress has a long and colorful history. In its natural state, it was covered with virgin timber—white pine and hemlock— and thick undergrowth. The ground was swampy, and a high water table and surface springs fed small streams draining the surrounding land. Gideon Putnam took the initial steps to make the uninviting area around the Congress accessible to the public, but Dr. John Clarke began major improvements when he acquired ownership in 1826. Most of Clarke's initial energy was put into bottling the water and taming the land. For years it remained in a primitive state, far from the picturesque setting it would become. Time, energy, foresight, and success in marketing the bottled water were all that Clarke needed to create the enduring park. By the mid-1830s, it was already a charming site. To complement the times and honor the spring, a classic Greek Revival temple was built over the Congress. Later, a pleasing Grecian pavilion was erected to shelter Clarke's Columbian Spring. Gathering crowds flocked to the springs, and pleasant rambling paths throughout the grounds provided opportunities for patrons to rest, relax and recover.

Ownership of the Congress passed to family and business associates after Clarke died in 1846. As the resource continued to increase in popularity, the water was bottled under the name Clarke and White. During that era, the Congress pavilion was altered by erecting additional columns and arched supports. The change doubtlessly aided in enclosing the pavilion in the winter when the bottling operation took the place of the summer crowds. In 1865, the famous spring was taken over by the newly-formed Congress and Empire Spring Company, largest and most successful of the area operators, controlling a major portion of Saratoga's mineral water business. In 1866, the company entered into a long-term contract with Hotchkiss and Sons, a Connecticut firm, giving Hotchkiss exclusive sale of the waters. To meet the supply requirements, the Congress and Empire Spring Company purchased the Granger glassworks and moved the bottle factory closer to the village that year. The arrangement with Hotchkiss was somewhat successful, but to gain better control of his own future, Hotchkiss bought shares of the water company and eventually gained control of it.

Throughout the ten years immediately following the Civil War, the Congress was visited by many thousands of guests. Few changes were made to the park, and it remained much as it had been for many years—a timeless classic setting—but, close by, a rapidly changing world had left its mark. Magnificent new hotels, homes and businesses were at the park's doorstep, displaying the more fanciful and elaborate architecture of a new era.

With the nation's centennial fast approaching, the trustees of the Congress and Empire Spring Company met in the summer of 1875 and approved plans to create a new Victorian version of their park. Drawing from his experiences in Paris, where he had been involved in other business pursuits, Hotchkiss came up with the idea of enclosing the grounds and creating an arcade entrance. That fall, work began which would transform the Grecian setting into a new, High Victorian Gothic wonderland. The final product was no less than stunning, though some would rue the passing of the time-honored pavilions. On Broadway, an elaborate, new, colonnaded entranceway connected Congress and Columbian Springs. Guests were welcomed, but now had to pay a small admission price to use the park. (Mineral water, however, was still free for the asking.) Everywhere throughout the colonnade, decorative embellishments, stained glass and brightly-painted woodwork proudly proclaimed its Victorian Gothic character. Equally stunning were the grounds of the park, beautified and enhanced by many plants, flowers and decorative embellishments. The park gave a new sparkle to Saratoga's crown, and its owners prospered, despite the fact that the cost and upkeep of the new park far exceeded what had been planned. Enjoyed in quiet solitude by individuals, and with great pomp and pageantry by huge gatherings, the park was considered by many to be the most picturesque and pleasant place found in Victorian Saratoga.

For the visitor not yet acquainted with the Congress and its park, what would it be like? What wonderful place was waiting?

Congress Spring is more generally known and used than any other Saratoga springs, and has probably effected more cures of the diseases for which its waters are a specific, than any other mineral spring in America. ... The medicinal effects of Congress Water have been tested for nearly a century, and its use is prescribed by physicians, with the utmost confidence. ... [In] a recent analysis of Congress, Prof. C.F. Chandler remarks that "the superior excellence of this water is due to the fact that it contains, in the most desirable proportions, those substances which produce its agreeable flavor and satisfactory medicinal effects—neither holding them in excess nor lacking any constituent to be desired in this class of water." ... Genuine Congress water is sold only in bottles. In this form it is sent to almost every part of the world, and its name is a household word. ... Congress Spring Park comprises almost the entire plot of ground encompassed by Broadway, Congress and Circular Streets. Originally a forest, possessing many natural attractions, it has been materially improved by grading, draining, and the addition of many architectural adornments, until it now presents a most beautiful appearance, and is one of Saratoga's principal charms. During the year 1876 the Congress and Empire Spring Co. expended nearly $100,000 on these improvements, and now it surpasses all other parks of equal size in the United States in the beauty of its graceful and artistic architecture. ... The grand entrance is at the junction of Congress Street and Broadway, near the Grand Union Hotel and Congress Hall on what is now called Monument Square. ... On entering turn to the right and you may pass through a short colonnade to the graceful spring-house over the Columbian Spring, or from the entrance turn to the left through the longer colonnade, and you come to the interior of the artistic pavilion over Congress Spring. ... Passing down a few steps and along the colonnade, you reach the ele-

gant cafe, where hot coffee and other refreshments may be obtained at reasonable prices, and may be partaken of while listening to the park music and enjoying the charming view of the lakes and the grounds. ... You may stroll at will, visiting the lake and shaded lawns, and listening to the delightful music of the very celebrated park band, which plays morning, afternoon and evening. In the evening the Band occupies the very unique and artistic Music Pavilion in the center of the lake. ... In the park, amid the flowers and shrubs, strolling over the grass-covered, shaded lawns, or lounging under the grand old forest trees, enchanted by the charming music—here it is that one may enjoy the supreme delights of a genuine rural summer resort. Every convenience for the park enjoyment is here afforded, including abundant settees and shade, and the security of efficient police supervision. The grounds are thoroughly lighted by gas at night, rendering them available as a place of evening resort. The scene in the evening, on the occasion of one of the grand concerts, is remarkably brilliant and charmingly fascinating. ... Admission to the park is regulated by tickets, for which a nominal charge is made. Single admission tickets, admitting to all except the evening concerts, 10 cents each."

CONGRESS SPRING BIRDSEYE VIEW
Photographer—P.H. McKernon, Saratoga

For untold millennia, a tangle of brush, giant trees, wild animals and every kind of crawling creature imaginable called this swampy basin its home. Civilization, in a relatively few years, wrested the area away from nature and created this picturesque setting. The handsome cover for the Congress fountain was built in the mid-1830s, a time when Greek Revival architecture was popular throughout the country. There was a classic simplicity to the Doric style, and the pavilion complemented the tone that characterized Saratoga in the years before the Civil War. This birdseye view from the late 1860s was likely taken from atop the Crescent Hotel located across Broadway from the park.

COLUMBIAN SPRING

Photographer—unknown, probably George Stacy, NYC

A large group patiently posed in front of the Columbian Spring, just a few feet from the park bandstand. Taken near the close of the Civil War, this view shows the stovepipe hats which were popular during the Lincoln era. With the assassination of the president and the coming of a new era, the hats, seen so often in earlier times, lost fashion by the 1870s.

BANDSTAND IN CONGRESS PARK
Photographer—unknown, probably George Stacy, NYC

Congress Park owner Clarke had astutely recognized there was money to be made in giving some things away for free. Villagers and guests could take the water at his spring, enjoy a lovely park with rambling walkways, and listen to music—all without charge. The crowds gave his Congress recognition and importance, and the musical entertainment helped attract and maintain the gatherings. The small bandstand is believed to be the very first of a number of park bandstands erected in the nineteenth century. Clarke appropriately placed it between his Congress and Columbian Springs, nestled against the little hill just to the south. Incidentally, the stereoview from which this early picture is taken has a two cent US revenue stamp affixed, indicating it was sold between September 1, 1864, and August 1, 1866. During that period, all photographs were taxed as luxuries to support the huge national debt incurred financing the Civil War.

LINCOLN'S BUST IN CONGRESS PARK
Publisher—G.O. Brown and Co., Baltimore, MD

A fine marble bust of President Lincoln sits atop a stone pedestal in Congress Park and was surely admired by patriotic citizens in the post-war years. The statue was probably placed here as a memorial shortly after the President's death in 1865, replacing a marble-winged cupid that had occupied the spot. For some unknown reason, however, Lincoln disappeared from the scene by the early 1870s. In the photo, a park attendant sweeps the pathways behind the protective fence. The Columbian Spring pavilion is in the background; beyond are commercial storefronts on Broadway.

HAY PILES, CONGRESS PARK

HAY WAGON, CONGRESS PARK
*Publisher—G.O. Brown and Co., Baltimore,
MD*

Had these two wonderful photographs not been identified, surely they could be mistaken for a farm scene with family and friends dressed in their Sunday best. The rural setting is, in fact, Congress Park, right in the middle of busy Saratoga. Taken only a few yards from the Congress Spring in the open area of the park, the views look east and southeast between the small sloping hills in the park. Workmen were likely hired to clear the tall grass in the park, and the cuttings were probably carted off to a local stable. Surely, most of the people pictured here were passing tourists who obliged the photographer by posing for the scene. With the view secured on a glass plate, the photographer doubtlessly encouraged some in the group to purchase a print as a reminder of their stay in Saratoga.

CONGRESS SPRING AND BOTTLING HOUSE
Publisher—G.O. Brown and Co., Baltimore, MD

Looking to the north, the photographer gives a different perspective on the Congress Spring. Taken circa 1870, the buildings immediately across the street contain the offices and bottling works of the Congress and Empire Spring Company. Clarke's successors had sold their holdings to this new company around the time of the end of the Civil War. During the off season, employees actively carried on the bottling operation here, filling and packing boxes of bottles and marking them for destinations like nearby Albany and far-off San Francisco. The company bottled water only from November through May, since at other times patronage at the spring put a heavy drain on the resource. During the winter, the bottling often went on around the clock. Note in this view the small sign on the side of the bottling house. It references the company's New York City office, "New York Depot 94 Chambers Street." Another camera stands ready near the spring and was probably set up by the same photographer to be used for group shots in front of the spring. Photographers were kept busy by such trade.

CONGRESS SPRING AND THREE GRAND HOTELS

Photographers—Baker and Record, Saratoga

This charming view captures a brief window in time when visitors gazed in wonder at three magnificent Victorian hotels on Broadway overlooking the Congress Spring site. From left to right stands Grand Central, Grand Union and Congress Hall. This view was likely taken in the summer of 1874 just before a tragic fire destroyed the short-lived Grand Central Hotel on October 1st. The small deer is likely from a deer shelter maintained on the park grounds.

CONGRESS SPRING AND CONGRESS HALL HOTEL
Publisher—G.O. Brown and Co., Baltimore, MD

Congress Hall towers majestically over the spring which gave it its name, and the view provides a dramatic display of two different periods in Saratoga's history.

The lovely circa 1870 scene shows a small group at the classic spring site while, at the same time, they are but a few feet away from Victorian opulence.

DEDICATION OF THE CIVIL WAR MONUMENT
Photographers—Baker and Record, Saratoga

On September 21, 1875, this large gathering met to dedicate a monument honoring local citizens who had formed the 77th Regiment during the Civil War. Throughout that day, parades, celebrations, and memorial services took place in the village. From the small platform, speakers detailed the commendable service and sacrifices of the unit. On hand with former members of the 77th were other veterans who had served in the 30th and 115th Regiments, as well as in artillery, cavalry and navy commands. Mustered in at Saratoga in the fall of 1861, the ranks of the 77th came from Saratoga, Essex and Fulton counties. The Regiment participated in many important battles while assigned to the Sixth Corps with the Army of the Potomac, and later at Fort Stevens and in the Campaign of the Shenandoah Valley. When they left Saratoga in '61, the unit numbered about 860 troops. Before the war's end, over 1400 men served in the unit. One in five died in battle or succumbed to disease. Many more spent long periods recovering from wounds, amputations and debilitating afflictions. The monument was placed in this prominent spot on Broadway to honor the courage of these men and to remind everyone of the sacrifices they made to preserve the Union. On the speaker's platform, just behind the flag-draped table on the right, sits a mustached Col. Winsor French, who led the troops through most of the war. Local photographers Baker and Record immortalized this scene for future generations by taking a large photographic plate during the ceremony. Copies were ready by the next day and offered by the firm for one dollar. This photo is of additional importance because it undoubtedly is one of the very last ever taken showing the original Congress Spring pavilion. A few days after the monument ceremony, the Congress and Empire Spring Company began to dismantle the structure to begin creating their new Victorian colonnade and entrance to the park.

ORIN P. RUGG

Photographer—unknown

A handsome Orin P. Rugg poses with his Civil War uniform and officer's sword, early in 1864. Rugg was born in Saratoga Springs in 1838, and worked in a dry goods store on Broadway before the war. In September, 1861, the 23-year-old Rugg enlisted in the 77th Regiment, and two months later left Saratoga to defend the Union. He showed exceptional ability as he rose through the ranks, making captain by December, 1862. On August 8, 1862, he wrote home and described the action and suffering. He ended the letter by writing " remember me to all my friends round about Saratoga. I would like a drink of Empire Water to night ..." Rugg witnessed many tragic battles over the course of the war. He saw too many Saratoga comrades carried off to field hospitals and buried in hastily-prepared graves. Orin was more fortunate than some of his friends at Antietam, Fredricksburg, Marye's Heights and The Wilderness. In May, 1864, Spotsylvania Court House was the next stop on the battle trail. On May 12, the men of the 77th were a small contingent among thousands of Confederate and Union troops engaged in an area known as the "Salient." Bodies fell and piled high, as fierce hand-to-hand combat raged all day in the rain. During the long nightmare, a fateful shot pierced Orin's chest. Stretcher bearers reportedly jumped in to carry him off to a field hospital, but he died along the way. The proud, handsome Captain was buried on the field. Six weeks later his only child, Orin Jr., was born. After the war, in the fall of 1865, Rugg's body was disinterred and returned to Saratoga where he was laid to rest at Greenridge Cemetery.

CONGRESS PARK, VICTORIAN BIRDSEYE VIEW

Photographer—Wm. Sipperly, Mechanicville and Schuylerville, NY

Over the years, success in marketing Congress Water had allowed its owners to provide and improve a picturesque park around the spring. In July, 1875, when the trustees of the Congress and Empire Spring Company met, they approved plans to totally redesign the park to create a Victorian setting more in keeping with the changing character of the village. Ambitious plans were laid out and by the first week of October workmen were already busy dismantling the old Congress pavilion. As the small temple came down, a newspaper account likened the scene to an ancient Greek ruin. Many were saddened. An enclosed shelter was built over the site to allow workmen to keep busy during the winter constructing the foundation for the planned arcade. Discarded wood from the old pavilion was neatly stacked and, in the cold months, served as fuel for the stoves which heated the temporary shelter. The plan called for considerable work on the grounds throughout the park as well. Just south of the park, on Broadway, construction on the new Windsor Hotel had also just commenced, and excavation of its foundation and basement provided vast quantities of fill needed in the park. On one day alone, November 21, 1875, it was reported that 22 shovelers and 22 teams of horses delivered 630 loads of fill to the park from the Windsor Hotel site. With pick and shovel other workers began to create a small lake in the park, while more workmen brought in loads of clay from nearby Red Spring to line it. By January 1876, skaters were already enjoying the ice on Saratoga's tiny new lake. The old Columbian Pavilion was finally razed in mid-April and, by the end of that month, 175 workers were busy throughout the property. Many worked on the new colonnade, but the richness of embellishments all around the park required considerable energies as well. Every effort was made to prepare the park for the beginning of the 1876 centennial summer season. In this view of the completed arcade, Congress Spring is under the high-peaked roof to the left, and Columbian Spring is in the portion at the right.

ENTRANCE TO CONGRESS PARK
Photographers—Baker and Record, Saratoga

The main entrance to the park was here, just off Broadway. Though visitors would now have to pay a small admission price to use the park, spring water was still free for the taking. Admission tickets were fifteen cents the first summer, but the fee was dropped after the summer season, late in September, for the locals. By the following summer, regular fare was reduced to ten cents. When the Civil War memorial was dedicated in September, 1875, it stood at the edge of the Congress Park property. However, in constructing the new entrance to the Victorian park, the street corner was rounded, which had the effect of placing the monument on Broadway. The spot was referred to as Monument Square.

VIEW FROM INTERIOR OF ARCADE
Photographers—Baker and Record, Saratoga

Once inside the Gothic colonnade, visitors looked out and saw this picturesque scene. Along with the beautiful setting, the Congress and Empire Spring Company began to offer a variety of entertainment and services. Visiting families especially appreciated the new "Children's Hour" held at four o'clock each day. Parents could safely surrender their children any afternoon for an hour of special fun.

FIRST GLIMPSE OF CONGRESS PARK

Photographers—Baker and Record, Saratoga

Passing through the entrance of the arcade, visitors caught this first pleasant glimpse of the park. The tall Victorian urn is one of a number of pieces of decorative iron-work cast in England and placed here in the park during the spring of 1876. The urn was created so as to represent the highly-touted bas relief figures, "Morning" and "Night" sculpted by Danish artist Thorvaldsen earlier in the 19th century. Placed just inside the park entrance, and constructed so as to be turned or rotated daily, the urn was to represent or suggest to visitors the time of day as they came upon the scene.

CONGRESS SPRING ARCADE

Photographers—Baker and Record, Saratoga

Entering the park and looking back at the colonnade, the visitor was amazed by the kaleidoscope of color: decorative iron work, stained glass windows, intricate woodwork, interesting shapes and lines, all brilliantly painted and all topped by a colorful slate roof. Beyond the arcade are the Grand Union and Congress Hall hotels.

VIEW FROM THE PARK LAKE

Photographer—Wm. Sipperly, Mechanicville and Schuylerville, NY

The small lake excavated during the project provided still more opportunities for decorative adornment. The new arcade extended beyond the Congress Spring right down to the lake, and in this view a wonderful scene was created by the reflection on the water.

FRESH WATER SPRING

Photographers—Baker and Record, Saratoga

This cast-iron fountain provided thirsty visitors an opportunity to drink fresh water. Doubtless, many who had not acquired a taste for the village's mineral spring water appreciated the so-called "Deer Spring." This fountain, along with the tall Thorvaldsen vase and four smaller iron urns, were reportedly molded in London as superior work of this quality was not then available in this country.

RESERVOIR IN CONGRESS PARK

Photographers—Baker and Record, Saratoga

The circular structure in the foreground was known as the Congress Park reservoir and was a very popular spot inside the park. Cut stone and decorative cast iron surround a small pool of water, and Victorian urns containing beautiful greenery sit atop the limestone pedestals. Ground water was channeled into the reservoir and there was a constant flow of water in and out which kept it fresh. Trout stocked in the reservoir could be admired in the crystal clear flow. This reservoir was created near the site of the old tall water tower erected by John Clarke many years earlier.

RESERVOIR AND PARK

Photographers—McDonnald and Sterry,
Albany and Saratoga

Benches and chairs all along the park walkways encouraged conversation and restful contemplation of the park's beautiful setting. This pleasant scene from the early 1880s shows the park reservoir in the foreground and the Congress arcade beyond. Rooms at the south end of Congress Hall, seen here in the background, provided a spectacular birdseye view of the park.

MUSIC PAVILION

Photographers—Baker and Record, Saratoga

The music pavilion at lakeside was a charming example of Victorian decoration and was used by the park band during their evening concerts. The colorful scene was especially attractive when illuminated by gaslight, and later by electricity. Surface water and ever-present drainage problems in this area made it fairly easy to scoop out the lake. This beautiful scene would one day be dismissed as Victorian excess by a future generation.

HALL'S BOSTON BAND, CONGRESS PARK

Photographer—unknown

Hall's Boston Band spent many summers at Saratoga performing at hotels and entertaining here in Congress Park. Music filled the park each day of the season, courtesy of park owners. The schedule generally included daily concerts, held mornings from 7:30 to 9:30 am, afternoons between 4 and 5 pm, and evenings from 8 to 10 pm.

CONGRESS PARK FOLIAGE

Photographers—Baker and Record, Saratoga

Gardeners were constantly busy caring for the plants in Congress Park. Here, some visitors pose in the luxuriant greenery. When the new park opened in 1876, the foliage was pleasant, but with growth through the years, it became ever more lush and beautiful. Evenings in the park were just as beautiful as the days as gas lamps along the paths lent a wonderful charm to the surroundings.

INTERIOR, CONGRESS PARK ARCADE

Photographers—Baker and Record, Saratoga

The inside of the arcade was a visual delight, a feast for the eyes with colored glass panels, rich slate flooring, and a seemingly endless variety of decorative woodwork. Victorian gas fixtures hang from the ceiling. Throughout the setting, Victorian hardwood chairs and walnut tables were available for the visitor's use. Just to the left of this group, by the leaded glass panels, Congress Spring water was provided for the asking.

INTERIOR, CONGRESS SPRING
Photographers—Baker and Record, Saratoga

In this beautiful setting, Victorian travelers were served Congress Water. Colorful leaded glass panels form the wall behind the counter where the dipper boys were stationed to provide the celebrated water. A chain and pulley mechanism on the back wall was used to bring up the water, replacing long poles with glasses on the end previously used by dipper boys.

CONGRESS PARK CARAMELS
Photographers—Baker and Record, Saratoga

H. Voullieme was a Saratoga confectioner who sold his well-known caramels here in the Congress Park arcade. Dressed in his baker's uniform, Voullieme looks every bit the part of a French pastry chef. The small cafe concession was located at the east end of the colonnade and, in this wonderful view, flags and a cloth sign frame the setting, with his showcases filled with tasty treats. Voullieme's main shop was on Broadway, under the Adelphi Hotel, where he sold manufactured confections, soda water, ice cream and a selection of imported precious stones, jewelry and minerals.

COLUMBIAN SPRING OVERVIEW
Photographers—McDonnald and Sterry, Albany and Saratoga

At the opposite end of the colonnade from Voullieme's cafe was the pavilion for the Columbian Spring. This overview, looking in a northwesterly direction, also shows a few Broadway stores which catered to the tourist trade. These shops were built on ground left vacant after the Grand Central Hotel was consumed by fire in 1874. The southern exposure of the Grand Union Hotel on Congress Street is in the background.

COLUMBIAN SPRING

Photographers—Baker and Record, Saratoga

This late-1870s view shows a closeup of the Columbian Spring. Though a charming setting, the Columbian was not as important as its neighbor, the Congress, and therefore did not have an elaborate structure like that found over the Congress.

H. VOULLIEME,
Manufacturer of Rich and Choice Confections,
ICE CREAM, SODA WATER AND FRUIT ICES.
CONGRESS PARK CARAMELS A SPECIALTY.
GENERAL DEPOT FOR VOULLIEME'S CONGRESS PARK CARAMELS.
Also, importer of Precious Stones and Jewelry, Onyx, Cameo, Amethyst, Blood Stone, Smoked Topaz, Calcedony, Amber, Lapis Lazuli, Agate, Cornelian, Malachite, etc. Splendid Specimens in the rough state.

No. 361 Broadway, Saratoga Springs, N. Y.

DEER LODGE

Photographers—Baker and Record, Saratoga

Built with cedar wood brought up from Peekskill, New York, this structure in the back of Congress Park was home for deer. The shelter, constructed in the Adirondack rustic style popular at the time, was undoubtedly a favorite spot for children. Deer had been kept at the park for many years. Col. Walker R. Johnson, who managed the entire Congress Spring operation, including the spring, bottling plant and park, for 34 years, was said to be particularly fond of 'his' deer. Somewhat tamed by the nature of their care, the deer were occasionally allowed freedom to wander outside the enclosed area shown, especially during the slow season. An unidentified caretaker is apparently feeding them in this view.

CHAPTER 6
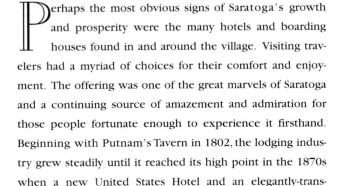

THE PRIDE OF THE COMMUNITY
Hotels and Boarding Houses

Perhaps the most obvious signs of Saratoga's growth and prosperity were the many hotels and boarding houses found in and around the village. Visiting travelers had a myriad of choices for their comfort and enjoyment. The offering was one of the great marvels of Saratoga and a continuing source of amazement and admiration for those people fortunate enough to experience it firsthand. Beginning with Putnam's Tavern in 1802, the lodging industry grew steadily until it reached its high point in the 1870s when a new United States Hotel and an elegantly-transformed Grand Union Hotel opened their doors to become the epitome of palatial Victorian lodging. Fundamental to the success of the village, the hotels were the pride and glory of the community.

Few communities in the country could match the diversity of Saratoga's hotels, which ranged greatly in the beauty of the grounds, the types of services provided, and in sheer physical size. Had almost any one of Saratoga's smaller guest houses been built in any other comparable community in America, it would have been considered a very large hotel. Buildings the size of the Adelphi and the Waverly Hotels, which advertised accommodations for 200 and 150, respectively, would have been considered palatial. Yet here, these wonderful smaller houses could accommodate barely a tenth the number the largest houses were capable of serving. Although no detailed, accurate inventory of the hotels and boarding houses was ever taken, references in guidebooks and directories give an indication of just how extensive the offerings were. Colt's guide from 1871 suggests that the hotels and boarding houses contained about 7800 rooms. The 1880/81 Boyd's Directory lists 33 hotels and 81 boarding houses. The 1882 Taintor's guide lists 60 establishments, advertising total accommodations for over 11,300 guests.

In the High Victorian years, the best known and largest of the Saratoga hotels were the Grand Union, the United States Hotels, and Congress Hall. Each was surrounded by a landmark Saratoga piazza filled with rockers, benches and

chairs. People would often debate which was the biggest or the best, and the issue is still debatable though, from the standpoint of size, the Congress always lost out, being in fact somewhat smaller than the other giants.

While the big three struggled at the top, many fine smaller hotels and boarding houses picked up their share of the trade during the excitement of the Saratoga season. These houses were located throughout the village, some amid the hustle and bustle of Broadway, others further away. They came in all sizes, accommodating anywhere from a few guests to a few hundred. They catered to persons seeking a quieter and less hectic environment, or more personalized and specialized services. A few proclaimed a temperance policy, or offered water cures to attract boarders. But most often, it was the generally more affordable rates which served to entice customers. Each house, in some way, secured its fortune by finding its own niche, and no room in the village was empty during the season. An especially admirable characteristic of Saratoga's hotels was the "no expenses spared" approach to the ease and enjoyment of patrons. The largest hotels provided specialty shops with exotic imported goods, bowling alleys, billiard rooms and barber shops, and organized a full array of daytime and evening activities. Musical entertainment was a standard offering. Bands and orchestras from New York and Boston traveled to the Springs to entertain throughout the entire summer season. Spacious parlors and huge ballrooms were filled with activity, and the larger hotels held dazzling grand balls every week. Guests dressed in elegant gowns and handsome suits scurried from one to the other to see and be seen. Monumental dining rooms seated thousands of guests at a time. An army of ever-diligent waiters spread impressive culinary spectacles before them each meal, every day of the week.

Plenty of employment opportunities existed to provide all the varied services. Local residents and workers from nearby towns took many jobs but, to operate efficiently, hotel managers also brought in help from the cities. Orchestra members, chefs, waiters, supervisors and bookkeepers often followed managers as they made seasonal moves to and from Saratoga.

Many hotels and boarding houses were open for the season only. Each May, crews began readying for the coming summer. Once open, the season started off slowly with guests trickling in during the early days of June. A month later, all the houses were packed. One guidebook of the period suggested June as an opportune time to visit; there were no crowds yet at the hotels and springs, and prices throughout the village were lower than they would be a month later. The guide went on to point out, however, that it was precisely the crowds and the "perpetual festival" of the Saratoga social experience that drew most visitors. The season continued into September, but by the third week of that month most places were closed. Following a few weeks of work by local carpenters, the great houses were boarded up for the winter. During the remainder of the year, they lay dormant except for necessary maintenance and alterations.

With growing crowds and prosperity, owners and management frequently had to expand their houses and offer more services to stay competitive. This was especially true in the post-Civil War Victorian years. The Saratoga season was short. A year's income had to be made in barely three months. Everything possible was done to attract patrons, and healthy competition among owners fueled the pursuit of ever-more-lavish and commodious houses.

Saratoga's early boarding establishments had been built and managed primarily by proprietors relying on their own means and hard work. But by the 1860s, it had become a common practice for one firm to erect a hotel and then lease it to a management company which actually carried on the day-to-day business. Few establishments (most notably the smaller houses) were actually owned and operated by the same firm or individual during this era. The frequent turnover of property and leases made it sometimes difficult to keep track of who owned, and who ran, a particular establishment. As one company made a fortune, another might fail and end in bankruptcy. The potential for prosperity, however, meant that there were always new owners and managers eager to step in and pick up the pieces.

There was always a close affinity between the hotels and the community. A sense of pride seemed to bind them. The hotel business was a popular topic in the local press, and the village was often abuzz with tales of the hotels and the deals that went on behind the scenes. Residents were keenly aware that "their" boarding establishments were in a large measure responsible for the overall success and well-being of the entire community. The great hotels might, in reality, be owned by wealthy people in far-off cities, but Saratogians felt a sense of ownership in them as well. After all, many Saratoga residents toiled in building, maintaining, and staffing them.

In anticipation of a stay in the village, what was the visitor to expect? What visions came to mind?

The hotels of Saratoga Springs are among the largest, most costly, elegant and comfortable in the world. For nearly a century people have journeyed to these springs, to drink their healing waters; and, as one day's visit is hardly worth the while, they have sought a home here during the summer season. It is this that has caused the village to open its door so freely, and to build up, from a small beginning, a system of hotels and boarding houses unlike anything else to be found. Added to this came, in time, the demands of the merely pleasure-seeking, fashionable world. People came to the springs for the sake of the gay company gathered here, and from year to year the hotels have grown, expanding their wings and adding room beyond room, till they cover acres of ground, and the halls and piazzas stretch out into miles. They have a bewildering fashion here of repeating the wondrous tale of these things. They talk about the miles of carpeting; the thousands upon thousands of doors and windows; the hundreds of miles of telegraph wires; vast acres of marble floors; and tons of eatables stored in the pantries, till one is lost in admirable confusion. It is all true, and that is the wonder of it. The management that governs it all is more remarkable than the gilding and mirrors. It is a sort of high science, unequaled in the world, combining the "ease of mine inn," and a perfection of detail in freedom from friction that is as pleasant as it is wonderful. ... Saratoga's face is her fortune, and it is said that the entire town devotes its days and nights to the comfort of the tourists. The tourist should be indeed happy. If he is not, it is safe to say it is his own fault.[8]

UNITED STATES HOTEL, BROADWAY
Photographer—Saratoga Photograph Co.,
Saratoga

On June 20, 1874, a magnificent new hotel opened on Broadway and was a source of immense pride for its owners and the village. Built of brick and stone and designed to accommodate 2,000 guests in single rooms and cottage suites, the United States Hotel was located in the very heart of the village where Division Street meets Broadway. The new building occupied space vacant since the devastating fire of 1865 took the hotel's predecessor. The new building and grounds were monumental, covering seven acres and containing over 900 guest rooms, including 768 sleeping rooms and 65 suites, each of which had a parlor and one to seven bedrooms. Standing four stories high (plus rooftop lookouts that were six stories high), with access via Otis elevators, the United States was lavishly appointed with carved walnut and marbletop furniture, elegant lace curtains, frescoed ceilings and decorative mirrors, chandeliers and artwork. For a number of years, it boasted being the only hotel in Saratoga that was thoroughly plumbed, having running water in all its guest rooms.

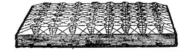

REAR ENTRANCE, UNITED STATES HOTEL
Photographer—unknown

Gazing east from Franklin Square, the back entrance to the United States Hotel appeared like this in the late 1870s. The smaller building in the distance, just to the left of the States, is the Arlington Hotel, also on Division Street. Out of view just to the left was the train station. Note a box car is parked on the tracks on the right side of the photo.

DIVISION STREET, UNITED STATES HOTEL

Photographer—Saratoga Photograph Co., Saratoga

The massive United States occupied a long block down Division Street, and in this photo the narrow piazza seems to cling precariously to its side. Built right next to the street, there was not much room on the walkway. Property was at a premium in this section of the village, and every square foot was used to its fullest potential. This section of the hotel was referred to as "millionaire's row." Each day of the season, as many as ten or twenty of the nation's richest men, including the Vanderbilts, met on the porch. Here they would talk horses, politics, parties, high finance and industry.

FRONT PIAZZA, UNITED STATES HOTEL

Photographers—McDonnald and Sterry, Mechanicville and Saratoga

The front piazza of the United States was a perfect spot from which to watch all the activity on Broadway. On the 232-foot porch, guests sat, rocked and took in the grand spectacle. Visible beyond the far end of the porch is a sign for the Arlington House.

UNITED STATES HOTEL FROM THE STREET
Photographer—T.J. Arnold, Ballston Spa, NY

At street level, the imposing front-stepped entrance and piazza of the United States could not possibly go unnoticed. It dwarfed the parade of people who daily made their way up and down Broadway. Those who climbed the steps and went inside walked upon a floor of white marble in the lobby. Farther up the street is the front corner of the Worden Hotel, formerly the Arlington. A note on the back of this photo indicates it was purchased in Saratoga on August 7, 1889. It was probably a cherished souvenir of some summer tourist.

MORNING SCENE ON REAR PIAZZA, UNITED STATES HOTEL
Photographers—Baker and Record, Saratoga

A huge, wonderfully dressed crowd gathered on the rear piazza of the United States Hotel reveals, in part, the essence of Saratoga during the Victorian days. The photographer captured a scene often encountered in Saratoga where the fine art of porch life reached its height.

LAWN VIEW, UNITED STATES HOTEL
Photographers—Baker and Record, Saratoga

An interior park-like lawn was created by
the encircling wings of the States. The grounds
were attractively laid out with walkways, trees,
shrubs, lawn statuary and fountains. The scene
was especially pretty at night when illuminated by colored lights and lanterns.

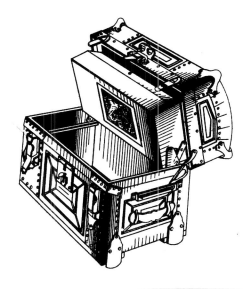

FOUNTAIN, UNITED STATES HOTEL
Photographer—unknown

This decorative embellishment was the
largest of the cast-iron ornaments on the lawns
of the United States. The hotel's north wing,
fronting Division Street, is on the left of the
interior courtyard.

DINING HALL, UNITED STATES HOTEL
Photographer—T.J. Arnold, Ballston Spa, NY
Waiters stand ready for guests in this 1880s view of the United States Hotel's dining room. The room was 52 by 212 feet, with 20-foot ceilings, and each table has been carefully covered and set with all the proper tableware and accessories.

Hotels required a huge staff to maintain operations. At the large hotels, the staff included many African-Americans who could work, but could not board, in the great houses on Broadway. Their employment was actively sought by management, and the workers often stayed in hotel-operated houses off, but near, the

hotel grounds. African-Americans worked primarily as waiters (as seen here), launderers and housekeepers. Smaller boarding houses, located primarily on the west side of the village, catered to African-American tourists and those unable to afford the high cost of a stay on Broadway.

PARLOR, UNITED STATES HOTEL

Photographers—Baker and Record, Saratoga

This comfortable setting shows a corner of the main parlor of the United States as it looked in the late 1870s. Like the other great hotels in the village, the States was filled with fine furniture, pier mirrors and elaborate hanging gas-light fixtures.

CONGRESS HALL HOTEL

Photographer—unknown

Built of brick with brown sandstone trimmings, Congress Hall was one of the pre-eminent hotels in Saratoga, and many considered it the most architecturally-pleasing of the Victorian giants. Built by Henry Hathorn and opened in 1868, it stood upon the site of Gideon Putnam's original Congress Hall which had burned to the ground in 1866. Shown here is the Broadway front with its promenade piazza. Three pavilions topping the mansard roof provided an ideal spot from which to view the whole village. The hotel had two wings in the back enclosing a small garden interior court. The place was perfectly suited for access to the mineral waters, with the Hathorn, Hamilton, Congress and Columbian Springs adjacent to the hotel. In the mid-1880s, the Congress advertised daily rates of $3.50 to $4.00, with a weekly stay ranging from $17.50 to $28.00. The lovely hotel was home to countless conventions and parties. Business, political, religious and social groups found the Congress an ideal location to gather.

FRONT PIAZZA, CONGRESS HALL
Photographers—Baker and Record, Saratoga
    Looking south, handsome columns line the porch in this mid-1870s view of the Congress. Carriages patiently await their next fare on Broadway.

YOUNG & LA MOUNTAIN,
Carriage Manufacturers & General Blacksmiths,
43 CAROLINE STREET,
SARATOGA SPRINGS, N. Y.

COMMODORE VANDERBILT, CONGRESS HALL PIAZZA
Photographer—Wm. Sipperly, Mechanicville & Saratoga
    A well-dressed group of men is gathered on the front piazza of Congress Hall, including the richest man in America, Commodore Cornelius Vanderbilt. Vanderbilt, who represented the epitome of wealth garnered from a growing industrialized America, sits among the group on the right, wearing the light-colored hat with black band. The Commodore enjoyed the races, gaming tables, and many parties offered in the unique summers of Saratoga. During the nineteenth century, wealthy and influential people found Saratoga the summer place to be, and the Commodore and a long line of his offspring were but a few of the many who gathered each year. Many of Saratoga's wealthy visitors went on to build their own palatial summer residences in the 1880s and '90s.

CONGRESS HALL BRIDGE

Photographers—Baker and Record, Saratoga

This bridge, built in June 1871, connected Congress Hall (shown at the far end) to the hotel ballroom across Spring Street, scene of many extravagant parties and grand balls. Two floors above the street, the bridge was often carpeted and decorated, thus creating a beautiful enclosed walkway between the buildings.

LOOKING WEST ON SPRING STREET, CONGRESS HALL BRIDGE

Publisher—Hall Bros., Brooklyn, NY

This view was taken from the bottom of Spring Street looking west. Congress Hall, on the left, is linked to its ballroom, on the right, by the unique bridge. Note the sign for Hathorn Spring on the right. In the background, across Broadway, is the northern front of Union Hotel. The Leland Brothers, owners of the Union at the time the bridge was built, had no wish for further competition with their own ballroom. They talked of an injunction to prevent Hathorn from building the bridge, undoubtedly arguing the bridge crossed public property. Perhaps they also thought it would be an eyesore for guests staying at the Union. But Hathorn wasted no time and completed the bridge while the Lelands could only complain.

COURTYARD, REAR OF CONGRESS HALL
*Publisher—G.O. Brown and Co., Baltimore,
MD*

    While views of the front of Congress Hall
are quite common, an early scene of the rear of
the hotel is seldom encountered. As this view
reveals, a two-level porch wrapped around the
small side wings of the hotel, providing a pleasant spot to sit and listen to the house band,
seen here at the rear courtyard.

REAR OF CONGRESS HALL
*Publisher—G.O. Brown and Co., Baltimore,
MD*

    This interesting circa 1868/69 view cap-
tures a scene rarely recorded during Victorian
Saratoga. Laundry days were filled with toil;
huge quantities needed to be cleaned daily. As
the village grew in the 1860s and '70s, large
parcels of undeveloped land were becoming
rare in the central part of the village, and little
room was available for this kind of activity. In
this scene, women hang sheets and linen in the
large vacant lot behind Congress Hall. By the
early 1870s, Hathorn erected a new laundry
building and stable on Spring Street, obviating
the need to hang sheets outside as shown
here. The commercial potential of such a photograph was limited and, in an era when nearly all cameras were in the hands of professional photographers, such scenes were seldom
taken.

INTERIOR OF CONGRESS HALL BALLROOM
Photographers—Hall Brothers, Brooklyn, NY

Magnificent Victorian chandeliers hang from the ceiling of the Congress Hall ballroom, which here appears to be a fairly sparse setting otherwise. Certainly a different scene was created, however, when the room was decorated and filled with guests. Bands, actors and orators entertained and enlightened from the stage at the end of this room.

JOHN H. WINDER,

Organist and Teacher of Music.

Pianos Forte Tuned.

392 Broadway, Saratoga Springs, N. Y.

UNION HOTEL

Photographer—D. Barnum, Boston and Saratoga

Coaches lining up on Broadway wait for their next departure from Union Hotel, owned by the Leland Brothers, during the summer of 1869. The name of Saratoga's first hotel was inexplicably changed from Union Hall to Union Hotel. Perhaps all the money the owners were putting into the old structure led them to want to distinguish its new offerings. The Lelands spent freely in the post-war years on both the inside and outside of the hotel. In fact, one year after this photo was taken, the old facade was a thing of the past, and a dramatic new Victorian version stood on Broadway.

COURTYARD LAWN, UNION HOTEL
Photographer—unknown

Saratoga's courtyards and gardens served as important social gathering places. From private conversations and restful naps, to huge parties and concerts, much seemed to happen on the great hotels' grounds. It is a mystery who the photo's subjects were in the scene at the Union—perhaps a mother and her five daughters here for the season.

UNION HOTEL, GROUNDS ENTRANCE
Photographer—P.H. McKernon, Saratoga

From Broadway, entrance to the grounds of Union Hotel park was gained through this gate. To the left of the gate was the front of Union Hotel, while to the right was the old Ainsworth Block section. The signs advertise entertainment held at the Leland Opera House, a new feature of the Union located at the rear of the grounds, directly ahead in this photo. The Opera House was scene to many gatherings and entertainments, from minstrel shows and theater productions to orchestra concerts and grand balls.

GRAND UNION HOTEL
Photographers—Baker and Record, Saratoga

A wave of new construction swept over Saratoga in the post-war years fueled by increasing numbers of tourists, changing tastes in architecture, and competition for the summer business. The Lelands heaped vast sums into the Union during 1870, creating the well-known edifice seen here, with its iron-columned piazza and mansard roof. Each year, it seemed, the Lelands were engaged in a spending frenzy, but eventually it caught up with them. Their troubles began in July, 1870—not in Saratoga, but in New York City. There, the Lelands leased and operated the huge Metropolitan Hotel which was owned by merchant Alexander Stewart. Because of dwindling patronage, the Lelands were unable to pay Stewart rent beyond June, 1870. They were forced into bankruptcy the following year in the face of rapidly accumulating debt. On September 19, 1870, a brief note in the *Daily Saratogian* foretold their problems. That morning, all of the Grand Union Hotel guests were unexpectedly sent off, bags and all, to other hotels in the village. The Lelands, "having urgent business elsewhere," suddenly shut down, closed for the season, and left town.[9] The Lelands returned the following year, however, and continued to improve the Grand Union. A New York City newspaper reported that Warren Leland had left for Saratoga with six tons of paint and six dozen paint brushes, intending to have the Grand Union painted inside and out. But with bankruptcy at hand, the Lelands ultimately lost their hotel. In the spring of 1872, Alexander Stewart paid $532,000 for the Saratoga landmark.

FRONT OF GRAND UNION HOTEL
Photographer—Aaron Veeder, Albany, NY

Alexander Stewart was a very successful New York City department store owner who had amassed a great fortune. Indeed, he was one of the richest men in the nation. Having been a summer patron at the Springs in the post-war years, he now used his fortune to leave his mark upon the scene. He commenced the monumental task of making the Grand Union even more modern and palatial. Improvements were made to drainage, heating, and ventilation systems, as well as to the kitchen. Many rooms were redecorated, and the ballrooms and front facade were newly adorned. Pictured here is the north front on Broadway, completed during the slow months between the 1874 and 1875 seasons. The iron-columned five-story exterior was rebuilt to complement the front constructed by the Lelands, thus eliminating what had been called the old Ainsworth Block section. With the work completed, the Grand Union now had an entire block-long front on Broadway between Washington and Congress Streets, all graced by a three-story piazza 800 feet long. During the next slow season, the winter of 1875/76, Stewart turned his attention to the south wing of the Hotel on Congress Street. The completion of that project would result in the Grand Union Hotel occupying almost an entire square block and having 2,400 feet of street frontage. When completed, the hotel accommodated up to 2,000 guests. Unfortunately, however, the great "new" hotel which Stewart's dream and wealth built was never enjoyed by its creator. In April, 1876, Stewart passed away. Although ownership remained with Mrs. Stewart, the Grand Union Hotel was taken over by Judge Henry Hilton, Stewart's attorney, who gained control of his friend's fortune and proceeded to spend it freely, here and elsewhere.

FRONT DESK/OFFICE, GRAND UNION HOTEL

Photographers—Baker and Record, Saratoga

Entering the Grand Union's front entrance, guests were greeted in this reception area and registered here at the front desk. An open rotunda extended to the top of the building, with balconies on each floor giving a view of the office and entrance below. The setting was beautiful, but there was an ugly side to this scene, at least for some. It was here at the Grand Union during the summer of 1877 that anti-Semitism began to be open-ly practiced by hotel management. Judge Henry Hilton, acting on behalf of the estate of the deceased owner, banned Jews from registering, even though Jews had been welcomed at the hotel in the past. The open prejudice was highly pub-licized because of the Grand Union's standing as the best-known hotel in the nation, causing an outrage across the country. Unrepentant, Hilton continued the practice, and Jews, along with African-Americans (who had also been exclud-ed), were turned away at this front desk.

Despite national criticism, the hotel's policy continued for 13 years, encourag-ing a few other establishments elsewhere to implement their own exclusionary policies. The incident seemed particular-ly out of character for Saratoga, a village which had long been considered a com-munity much more tolerant and recep-tive than most. Indeed, Jews turned away from the Grand Union Hotel found welcome signs but a few doors away in any direction, and along Broadway, suc-cessful shops and businesses were oper-ated by Jewish proprietors.

GRAND UNION HOTEL, OFFICE/LOBBY
Photographer—Aaron Veeder, Albany, NY

Guests entering the front door of the Grand Union surveyed this scene on the left side of the reception area. (The main desk was to the right of this view.) The doors in the back open onto the hotel's rear piazza and interior garden courtyard. The embellishments of the Victorian era can be seen everywhere, from floral decor molded along the supporting columns, to decorative gas lamps and prisms, to a lovely checkerboard floor of marble. Note the spittoons placed alongside each column on the floor. They were a necessary convenience for guests who "chewed".

DINING ROOM, GRAND UNION HOTEL
Photographer—George Conkey, Saratoga

Hotel staff pose for this 1880s view of the Grand Union Hotel's dining room. The huge room was even more spacious than the United States's, covering an area 60 feet wide by 275 feet long. The Grand Union had a staff of 250 African-American waiters, and required a huge support staff of cooks, bakers, busboys and dishwashers to keep the many guests well fed. During this period, the main meal was dinner, which was taken in the mid-afternoon when all guests were served at the same time. The multi-course feasts usually lasted two hours or more. Not a more enticing culinary spectacle could be found anywhere, and that's just the way the guests and hotel management wanted it. Cornelius Durkee, in *Reminiscences of Saratoga*, quotes from an old scrapbook the following quantities of food consumed at the Grand Union Hotel in a single day in the summer of 1872: "over 1200 quarts of milk from J.W. Eddy; 1500 pounds of beef from Ottman of Fulton Market, New York; 800 pounds of chickens from Syracuse and western New York; 200 quarts of berries from Plattsburg and northern points; 20 bushels of potatoes from the surrounding country; other vegetables in large quantities according to season."[10]

HOTEL PARLOR, GRAND UNION HOTEL
Photographer—Charles Bierstadt, Niagara Falls, NY

HOTEL PARLOR, GRAND UNION HOTEL
Photographer—T.J. Arnold, Ballston Spa, NY

These two views show how decorating styles changed at the Grand Union. The earlier view depicts a handsomely-furnished main parlor in the early 1870s. By the beginning of the 1880s, as the other view reveals, additional embellishment to the ceiling, hanging light fixtures and window treatments, as well as new carpeting and furnishings, are evident.

REAR PIAZZA, GRAND UNION HOTEL
Photographers—Baker and Record, Saratoga

In the middle of this crowd, gathered in the late 1870s, the hotel band entertains on the rear piazza of the Grand Union Hotel. This section of the piazza is but a small portion of what was said to be one solid mile of porch surrounding the building. The gentleman at the left sits on a cast-iron railed landing; these landings were attached to many of the hotel's second-story bedroom windows.

BAKER & RECORD,
PHOTOGRAPHERS,
Over Commercial Bank,
SARATOGA, N. Y.

ALL KINDS OF
PHOTOGRAPHIC WORK
Made at this Establishment.
Old Pictures Copied and Finished in Oil or Ink.

CHILDREN IN REAR GARDEN COURT OF THE GRAND UNION HOTEL
Photographers—Baker and Record, Saratoga

A few boys sit in the middle of a large group of well-dressed young girls in this view from the 1870s. We can only speculate on the significance of this party-like scene. It could well be one of the hotel's "activities of the day"—there were many for children's amusement. On the left, two seated women—perhaps nurses or nannies—hold the youngest children. Many wealthy guests brought servants to Saratoga to tend to their needs during the long summer season. Each year, thousands enjoyed activities at the Grand Union's courtyard park, but the 1879 season was especially memorable. That year, the old Leland Opera House had been removed, and the grounds were further embellished. But perhaps the biggest excitement was caused by the introduction of electric lighting in the park. Incandescent electric light now shone upon a festive scene, and guests marveled at the radiant light which would one day take the place of the park's gas lights and Chinese lanterns.

CRESCENT HOTEL

Photographer—D. Barnum, Boston and
Saratoga

At the southwest corner of Broadway and Congress Street stands the Crescent Hotel in this late 1860s view. Its name is boldly painted across the brick edifice which faces north toward the Lelands' Union Hotel, just across Congress Street. Crescent Hotel was erected on this site after a fire on July 4, 1864 destroyed the old Stanwix Hall, along with a number of other buildings. Stanwix Hall had been used for years by Dr. Hamilton for his popular medical establishment and hotel located on the property, called the Crescent Cure and Dr. Hamilton's Medical Institute. Hamilton erected the handsome Crescent Hotel in its place.

FRONT VIEW, CRESCENT HOTEL

Photographer—D. Barnum, Boston and
Saratoga

This closeup shows a group posed on the Broadway front of the Crescent Hotel. The Crescent had a small landing with cast-iron railing extending beyond its columned porch entrance from which boarders could gaze out across Broadway and see the crowds gathered at Congress Spring.

A sign advertises confections in the stores below; the giant watch which hangs at the left is also an advertisement. Note the photographs hanging alongside the doorway to the shop at the left below. This was where Deloss Barnum had his photo studio in the late 1860s. Here, Barnum took portraits and sold scenic views and stereoviews of the region. On October 1, 1871, the brick Crescent, along with many adjacent buildings, including the Park Place Hotel, burned to the ground.

GRAND CENTRAL HOTEL
Photographer—unknown

The demise of the Crescent and adjacent buildings led to the birth of another great guest house, the Grand Central Hotel. A number of pieces of property were consolidated after the great fire of October, 1871, and the owners, Charles Brown and Dr. Hamilton, erected this palatial Victorian structure to receive guests for the 1872 season. Furnished in an opulent high-Victorian manner, the hotel had both a front and rear piazza and boasted its own mineral spring. Crystal Spring water was served at the hotel and was available for sidewalk patrons from the counter seen here under the long awning at the left end of the building. The Grand Central could accommodate 1,000 guests at this prime Broadway location, and the firm of W.W. Leland and Company were given the lease to run the day-to-day operations. Leland had only a few months earlier lost his Grand Union Hotel, right next door. The Columbian Hotel, also recently rebuilt, is at the far left in this photo.

T. F. MAGOVERN,
(Successor to W. H. Baker.)

PHOTOGRAPHER,

446 Broadway,   Saratoga Springs, N. Y.

All negatives made by the old firm of Baker & Record and of W. H. Baker, on hand. The collection consists of over 50,000 negatives, which has taken over 20 years to accumulate. Duplicates of any of this collection furnished on short notice.

FRONT ENTRANCE, GRAND CENTRAL HOTEL
Photographer—unknown

Ghostly figures and blurs, the result of movement and a long exposure time, appear on the sidewalk and by the hotel steps in this view of the Grand Central. Note that, at the top of the stairway on the left, a photographer stands next to his tripod and stereo camera with its twin lenses. That photographer was undoubtedly taking porch-scene stereoviews like the following photo.

REAR PIAZZA, GRAND CENTRAL HOTEL
Photographer—unknown

Gilmore's Boston Band entertained mornings at ten o'clock on the rear piazza of the Grand Central. The Grand Central's size and appointments put it in a class with the top Saratoga hotels. Unfortunately, one of the hotel's owners, C. R. Brown, found himself in financial difficulties in 1873. Forced into bankruptcy when tenants failed to pay money due, he lost the hotel and was relegated to tenant himself, conducting his trade as a jeweler and optician in the magnificent building he helped create. Brown's partner in the project, Dr. Robert Hamilton, was in a better financial position and eventually sold his share to a buyer from Boston. The new owners had little time to enjoy their purchase, for at the end of its third summer season the beautiful hotel burned to the ground in October, 1874.

For the remainder of the century, this prime commercial site was the location of less grand ambition. Popularly known as the Grand Central Block after the great fire, it was occupied by small shops and commercial ventures, most of which perished in another great fire at the century's end.

COLUMBIAN HOTEL
Publisher—E. & H.T. Anthony, NYC

The Columbian Hotel was among a class of large hotels in the village that were pleasant and well-furnished, but were not of the palatial proportions of the biggest hotels. They were sought-out for the less hectic atmosphere and more personalized service they offered, but for many, it was the more affordable rates that led them to these smaller hostelries. This view, taken between 1872/74, shows the so-called New Columbian, built in 1872. An earlier, similar version was destroyed on this spot in 1871, but was quickly resurrected for the next season. During the winter of 1875/76, the building at the left was razed and the Columbian added a number of rooms. It was then said to accommodate up to 250 guests.

ARLINGTON HOUSE
Photographers—Baker and Record, Saratoga

At the intersection of Broadway and Division Street, was the Arlington, a handsome four-story brick structure capped by a mansard roof. Located in the middle of the village, its 300 guests were ideally situated for a short walk almost anywhere downtown. It was erected between the fall of 1865 and the summer of 1866, and replaced the old Marvin House which was consumed in the terrible fire of June, 1865. This building was initially known as the new Marvin House, but was subsequently renamed the Arlington Hotel when taken over by new proprietors in the summer of 1873. In 1885, the hotel was again taken over by a new owner, named Worden, who ultimately gave his name to the hotel.

KENSINGTON HOTEL

Photographer—T.J. Arnold, Ballston Spa, NY

The Kensington was a brand new hotel when it opened for the summer of 1882. It was a large first-class hotel capable of accommodating up to 400 people. Otis elevators took guests conveniently to all five floors of the brick building. Situated on Union Avenue between Circular and Regent Streets, the lovely hotel was located "off Broadway," but still near the main activity of the village. The back of Congress Park was diagonally across Circular Street from the Kensington. Vehicles heading out Union Avenue for the race course or Saratoga Lake passed the hotel.

WAVERLY HOUSE

Photographers—Baker and Record, Saratoga

The Waverly House, built just before the outbreak of the Civil War, was a small flat-iron-shaped hotel located at the northern end of Broadway's commercial district where North Broadway begins. Built in this shape to conform to property lines, the Waverly touted its homey modern furnishings and its quiet and pleasant atmosphere. It could accommodate 150 guests who surely enjoyed the two-level piazza surrounding the building and the excellent house orchestra which performed three concerts a day. On the first floor, in the front of the triangular building, Isaac Clapp operated a small grocery store. In 1882, a station was erected next to the Waverly to serve a brand new rail line that connected Saratoga with Mt. McGregor.

WINDSOR HOTEL
Publisher—Stereoscopic Gems of Saratoga

WINDSOR HOTEL, FRONT PIAZZA
Photographer—unknown

In early October, 1875, Mrs. Anne O'Donoghue of New York City announced plans to erect a new hotel in Saratoga on property she owned on Broadway just south of Congress Park below William Street. The parcel was a conspicuous and commanding spot overlooking the park and had a fine view of almost the entire village. The local architectural firm of Croff and Camp prepared the plans for the Italian-style building, and shortly thereafter, local builder D.M. Main began the construction. There was no time to waste between summer seasons, and that year the slow season in Saratoga was anything but slow. Major construction was taking place throughout the village in anticipation of the nation's centennial year and the expected tourists it would bring.

During November, foundation work was completed at the new hotel site, and in December the framing commenced. By the first week of January, the fourth floor was already taking shape. In mid-January, Mrs. O'Donoghue's son arrived in town to inspect the work being done on her behalf. While here, he announced that the hotel would be called the Windsor Hotel. By early February, the frame was completed, with the main cornice finished by mid-month. In early March, lathing was well under way; plastering started by the month's end. In April, the windows were all in place at the Windsor, and the interior doors were being hung. Meanwhile, outside, masons were busy at work laying the countless bricks needed to cover the huge building.

At the end of the month, tall columns were put into place to create a piazza across the entire north-facing side. During May, much of the finishing and decorating took place. Paint, wallpaper and finishes were applied. Rooms were measured and carpeting ordered. Ovens and ranges were installed in the kitchen, and furniture began to be placed throughout the hotel.

By the first of June, management was confident that they would open to guests by the 15th of the month. On the ninth, they finally received permission to erect street lamps in front of their hotel. (All but the one on the corner of Broadway would be the hotel's responsibility to erect, maintain and supply with gas—the village, after all, could only provide so much.) When it opened, the hotel's owner and all those who had worked on the building were proud of their accomplishment. In but eight months this well-appointed hotel had risen from a vacant lot and was capable of accommodating 300 guests in Victorian splendor and comfort.

WINDSOR HOTEL

Photographer—T.J. Arnold, Ballston Spa, NY

Despite all the hopes and expectations of its owner, the Windsor Hotel proved to be a financial disaster. Problems started almost immediately when the great hopes for an overwhelming wave of tourists during the nation's centennial year never quite materialized. The location seemed to be ideal, but its owner struggled during the short Saratoga seasons. Recognizing potential in the property, however, Judge Henry Hilton purchased it and set about redesigning and redecorating the Windsor. The Judge spent generously, producing a lovely building with sweeping wrap-around porches and a new main entrance on Broadway. It was packed full of fine-quality furniture, accessories and artwork, and became one of the most expensive houses to stay in at the time. Hilton's remake of the Windsor produced the only large hotel in Saratoga exhibiting the graceful lines of the popular late-Victorian, Queen Anne style. Management also sought to distinguish itself by employing an all-white staff. This distinctive feature was boldly proclaimed in its advertisements, appealing to the prejudices still prevalent in America.

DINING ROOM, WINDSOR HOTEL
Photographers—Record and Epler, Saratoga

PARLOR, WINDSOR HOTEL
Photographer—T.J. Arnold, Ballston Spa, NY

These two views show the handsome interior of the Windsor Hotel after Hilton redecorated it. In the dining room, Victorian walnut cane-seat chairs encircle tables neatly set with tableware. The parlor appears quite crowded with Victorian furniture and accessories, but this style of decorating is typical of the time. The Statue of Liberty casting portrays an image popular during the period, one that was replicated on everything from souvenir statues to beer bottles and patent medicines.

FRONT OF CLARENDON HOTEL
Publisher—E. & H.T. Anthony, NYC

PIAZZA OF THE CLARENDON HOTEL
Photographer—Sterry, Saratoga

The Clarendon Hotel opened on Broadway about 1860, evolving from an early structure operated as a boarding house. Located a short distance south of Congress Park on the west side of Broadway, the lovely Clarendon received many of the nineteenth-century social elite summering in the village. Behind the front of the Clarendon, a large five-level addition/wing housed many of its guest rooms. On the north side of the property beyond the piazza, a lovely garden park and the Washington Spring graced the hotel grounds. The tendency for hotel owners to create grander and more elaborate facades after the Civil War was resisted by owners of the Clarendon, and the charm of an earlier time was kept intact during those grand days of Victorian adornment. This scene shows the massive wood columns, clapboard exterior and shuttered windows so common in earlier times. Indeed, nineteenth-century historian Nathaniel Sylvester described it in 1878 as "the only hotel in Saratoga Springs which is painted white with green blinds."[11] But, by the early 1880s, ownership and management changes, occasional damaging but not disastrous fires, and the rigors of the competitive marketplace forced even the old Clarendon to finally update. The front section of the Clarendon was elevated to five stories, and the round Greek columns were replaced by thin soaring columns supporting a porch on the fourth floor. The hotel's 500 guests enjoyed new Otis elevators and an elegantly appointed cafe.

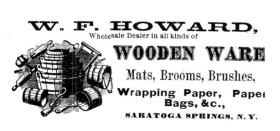

PARLOR, CLARENDON HOTEL
Photographer—Sterry, Saratoga

The parlor of the Clarendon did not display the decorative excesses of the other large hotels in the village. As shown in this late 1870s view, the hotel was tastefully furnished, with paintings on the wall and a piano ready for an entertaining tune adding to its special homey appeal.

CLARENDON HOTEL

SARATOGA SPRINGS, N.Y.

Harris & Losekam, Proprietors.

ED. P. HARRIS.   CHARLES LOSEKAM.

MANSION HOUSE

Photographers—Baker and Record, Saratoga

Mansion House was in a class of smaller hotels and boarding houses, most of which were capable of accommodating only 20 to 100 guests. Such places were frequently found outside Saratoga's downtown area, and therefore appealed to families or persons seeking a quieter stay. This mid-1870s view of the Mansion House shows guests posed outside the homey-looking structure, with its beautiful lawns and elm, maple and pine trees. The hotel was situated out Spring Avenue near Excelsior Park and was a short carriage ride from the village. The Excelsior, Union, Eureka and White Sulphur Springs were all close by. The Saratoga Lake Railway passed nearby, and a small whistle stop provided access via train after a line was laid in 1881. The Lawrence family, owners of the Excelsior Spring Company, built a sizable addition on the side of the original structure and renamed it the Excelsior Spring Hotel later in the century.

VERMONT HOUSE

Publisher—J.A. French, Keene, NH

Guests at the Vermont House obliged a photographer to capture this scene in the early 1870s. Taken in the hotel courtyard, this picture shows visitors playing croquet, a popular pastime during the Victorian era. Barely visible are the wickets and the mallets which some hold. The Vermont boarding house was operated by Benjamin and Clarissa Dyer, and advertised accommodations for 120. Located just off Broadway, on the corner of Grove and Front Streets, the large brick building was capped by a mansard roof and had this pleasant small courtyard behind it. In 1865, the Dyers, native Vermonters, came to the area and settled on a farm in Greenfield, just outside of Saratoga. But, in 1868, they turned to new pursuits and began working on this hotel. Benjamin was a deeply religious man who throughout his life was involved with reform movements against the evils of slavery and intemperance. His goal in building the hotel was to create a place for summer visitors which would be neat and comfortable, yet affordable, as well as quiet, orderly, and free from drinking and gaming. The Vermont House was well-patronized, and after Benjamin's death in 1877, his wife continued operation of the hotel for a number of years. In this scene, the Dyers sit on the porch just to the right of the middle post.

CHAPTER 7
AMUSEMENTS, EXCURSIONS AND EVENTS

Most Victorian summer travelers knew about Saratoga's refreshing springs, grand hotels and horse racing, but a wealth of other pleasures were also waiting. For those so inclined, one could easily research the offerings ahead of time by securing a tourist guidebook detailing the wonders of Saratoga. For the active traveler, the question was not what was there to do in Saratoga, but rather, how much could one possibly fit in during one's stay.

Stepping off the train, a world of opportunity seemed to suddenly unfold—only a few steps from the station was Broadway. A grand promenade of the rich and famous strolled up and down the main street, and anyone could fill idle hours enjoying the colorful spectacle. Signs, posters and handbills advertised amusements, theatrical productions, musical concerts and interesting shops.

Shopping was one of the celebrated pleasures of Saratoga. Places like Mark M. Cohn's "fancy goods" store lined Broadway during the Victorian era. At Cohn's, one could choose from a colorful assortment of ribbons, cashmere shawls, hosiery, parasols and the like, which made nice souvenirs or gifts for a loved one back home. The curious would perhaps find G. Miyamoto's summer store at the Grand Union Hotel an interesting place with its exotic assortment of imported Japanese goods. Across the street, at Congress Hall, for a number of summers Mrs. Wedel offered tourists worsted goods, embroideries and fancy baskets. The Palais Royal, up from their 5th Avenue, New York, store for the season, advertised fans from Paris and Vienna, as well as imported sash ribbons and lace goods. Souvenir stereoscopic views of Saratoga, fine stationery, books, and the latest newspapers from around the country were available at C. P. Penfield's Bookstore on Broadway. Countless other interesting shops lined the streets over the years.

But if shopping did not interest the traveler, then maybe a performance at the Putnam Music Hall on Phila Street would. The Hall was one of a number of venues in the Victorian years where a variety of troupes, operas and vocal groups performed. Opening in the summer of 1879 in the old Congregational Church, the Putnam's first draw was advertised as a curiosity show, a "two-headed nightingale" accompanied "by a tiny pair of Italian dwarfs."[12] Entertainment here and elsewhere in the village covered the entire range from sensational sideshow to serious operas with internationally-known vocalists. Saratoga was rarely without some special form of entertainment or attraction.

A stroll down Broadway in the 1880s led to the popular Saratoga Gallery of Fine Arts, where European paintings draped the walls. If the traveler didn't have the means to purchase a fine canvas, a visit would still serve as an interesting "museum" experience. North from the Gallery, the visitor could walk toward High Rock and visit a real museum operated by Dr. Haskins at the Seltzer Spring house. The museum's natural history specimens were on display, but, for the right price, the entire collection could be purchased.

Within easy walking distance of all the hotels were notable buildings and charming residential streets. A pleasant afternoon stroll along the shady avenues did much to add to the Saratoga experience. Interesting small shops operated by local merchants and tradesmen lined the streets and alleys off Broadway. On side streets like Phila, Putnam and Caroline, travelers would see bustling activity at shops, saloons, liveries, groceries and restaurants. Nationally-known financiers, politicians and artists were always out and about in Saratoga. Who knew where or when one might encounter a governor, visiting foreign dignitary, or Civil War general? Around the next corner might be a famous author, composer, or railroad tycoon.

Travelers with an itch to explore could leave the village on day or afternoon trips to nearby Saratoga Lake and other interesting places. The lake was an especially popular destination during the Victorian era, and its restaurants and boat rides were important parts of the Saratoga experience. Rowing competitions and intercollegiate regattas drew huge throngs. Day trips to Mt. McGregor, historic Schuylerville, and the Revolutionary War battlefields were also popular. The more venturesome tourists took longer excursions by rail and coach to places like Lake George and the rugged Adirondacks.

Nature lovers who wanted to stay near town had only to head out North Broadway and tour Judge Henry Hilton's property, Woodlawn Park. This was one of the large private estates in the area which were open to the public. Each was laid out with pleasant walks and picturesque settings. The fisherman needn't journey far from town either, wasting precious time traveling to secure his or her catch from some mountain stream. Gridley's Trout Ponds were located off Union Avenue, just past the Race Course. A few lazy hours spent casting for trout while swinging from a hammock did much to set the mind at rest.

Special sporting events, like the track and field meets or baseball games between visiting teams at the Glen Mitchell property, were very popular. Some of the events pitted the nation's best athletes and universities in intercollegiate competition. Trotting races at Glen Mitchell and other venues drew crowds and provided competition well beyond the summer seasons. Bowling alleys, rifle ranges and billiard halls offered an afternoon of fun and competition as well.

Saratoga was not just a place for individuals and families. It had long courted and attracted large groups, and during the post-war years, especially during the 1880s and '90s, Saratoga became a popular destination for organizations. The village was an ideal setting for conventions, reunions and special events. This trade was a healthy revenue-producer for shopkeepers and hotel owners, and as time went on, these gatherings were often held outside the usual summer season, thus adding significantly to the local year-round economy. Trade fairs, church groups, political parties, militia units, social clubs, collegiate athletes, all found the village a perfect place to meet. It seemed every organization imaginable, at one time or another, found its way to the Springs.

It may be said of Saratoga Springs that "its face is its fortune." Eight months in the year it lives in fond recollections of the last season, or in hopes of the next. June, July, August and September, it devotes to the solemn duty of entertaining its thousands of visitors. It may be a solemn thing for the natives, but for the visitors it is highly jolly. As its face is its fortune, the village, with great worldly wisdom, endeavors to wear as pretty a face as it can, and makes a special effort to entertain its company. The result is a gratifying success. The stranger, on arriving, at once asks for an "order of exercises." What are the proper things to do? how do you do them and what are the correct hours? The programme has never been printed, and the best that can be done is to refer to the charms of the place, as set forth elsewhere, and let the intelligent visitor take his choice. The first and most proper thing to do is to get up and go out before breakfast for a drink of spring water. Of course, one has duly consulted an MD in regard to this matter, and settled beforehand which spring is to be patronized. If this has been neglected, the chances are of receiving a vast amount of earnest and useless advice from innocents who have imbibed, and been cured of various prosaic complaints that they were heirs to from their youth up. The way these people rehearse their miseries, the touching tales they repeat of their disordered stomachs (as if any one cared for them), and the beautiful enthusiasm they display concerning their wonderful cures, make one of the minor amusements of Saratoga Springs. It may be safely called an amusement, for to every one but themselves their case is more funny than sad, more ridiculous than pathetic. One must be proof against these gratuitous advice givers, and learn to listen to their tales of woe with amused resignation and heroic neglect. Select your own spring, and never take the advice of anyone, unless it be your wife or medical man. Determined to have a good time, the visitor no sooner escapes the advice of the good-natured incapables than he takes his prescribed glass, and, in a thankful frame of mind, turns to see the others drink. Their ways are various—very. Some imbibe vast gobletfuls with a heroic smile; some sip from dainty cups, and try to make people think they like it—which isn't true. Others simply drink, and drink, and drink, till the spectator is lost in wonder, love, and praise to think they do not explode like a defective soda-fountain. Some call it delicious; others, horrid; and some don't drink at all, being timid withal. No place in the world will so bring out the likes and dislikes, weaknesses and small vanities of people, as a Saratoga spring early in the morning. To stand on one side and see the performance, serves as an exhilarant, and will make one good-natured for a half a day. This episode being over, one may return to the hotel for breakfast. By this time the morning meal acquires a wonderful interest. The waters act as a splendid stimulant to the appetite, and one is inclined to be particularly courageous with knife and fork. This, too, may be called a part of the amusement programme, for the filling of such a particularly fine multitude is a performance both entertaining and peculiar. When half a thousand people take coffee together, there is sure to be much that is original and amusing, and nowhere in the world are such gorgeous and multitudinous breakfasts served under one roof as at Saratoga Springs. Breakfast over, one may do as he pleases, with the most refreshing freedom— that is if you are a man. If not, an iron rule of conduct has been laid down for the ordering of your uprising and downsitting, goings out and comings in. This is the solemn formula announced by one of those awful authorities that rule the fashionable world. Every lady will read it with tears of gratitude when she thinks of the humiliating disaster its obedience will save her. "Rise and dress; go down to the spring; drink to the music of the band; walk around the park; bow to gentlemen; chat a little; drink again; breakfast; see who comes in on the train; take a siesta; walk in the parlor; bow to the gentlemen; have a little small talk with gentlemen; have some gossip with ladies; dress for dinner; take dinner an hour and a half; sit in the grounds, and hear the music of the band; ride to the lake; see who comes by the evening train; dress for tea; get tea; dress for the hop; attend the hop; chat a while in the parlors, and listen to a song from some guest; go to bed." The amount of wisdom involved in the above rules for conduct while in Saratoga is immense. See what delights, what charms of social intercourse; what heavenly pleasurings are spread before the lady visitor! Society is made for the young lady—and so is Saratoga. The sensible girl, the young woman with a mind of her own, laughs a scornful laugh at such folly, and does as she pleases with young American independence. She listens to the band if she wants to; she visits the Indians or the Circular Railway, or goes to Gridley's to fish the speckled trout in an armchair, or she does what she likes, and does not go to bed at all if there is a ball going on. Put ten thousand well educated people, with nothing to do and great skill in doing it, in half-a-dozen houses not half-a-mile apart, and, in the nature of things, there are good times in abundance. Small need of such a silly programme as the above, while half the village stands ready to amuse the visitors and all the visitors stand ready to amuse themselves. There are walks and drives, music and dancing, parties both small and great, hops every night, and a grand ball every week. There are excursions in every direction, and fifty thousand well-dressed people to see in a week. The wealth, brains, and culture of the country meet at Saratoga Springs, and one with

any grain of common sense can find abundance to do, to see, and to admire. There is no lack of social intercourse of the most refined and cultivated kind, and such absurd directions for conduct as we have quoted would be insulting if they were not so wonderfully silly.[13]

CIRCULAR RAILWAY
Photographer—D. Barnum, Boston and Saratoga

CIRCULAR RAILWAY, CLOSE-UP
Photographer—unknown, probably George Stacy, NYC

One of the more curious amusements in Saratoga Springs during the nineteenth century was the Circular Railway. This unusual self-propelled ride consisted of two circular tracks upon which ran small cars in opposite directions. Passengers hand-pumped a gear mechanism to move the vehicles along. The Circular Railway was originally located on the high ground of Congress Park beyond the spring. It was just off Circular Street near Park Place (shown here in both views), and was built at least as early as 1838. The railway was dismantled in the spring of 1871 and moved just north of Congress Street, along Circular, to become part of the Indian Camp and Park located there. By the early 1880s, it was again moved to a new location at another Indian Encampment off Ballston Avenue, about two blocks west of Broadway.

INDIAN ENCAMPMENT, ROW OF VENDOR TENTS
Photographer—D. Barnum, Boston and Saratoga

INDIAN ENCAMPMENT, CLOSE VIEW
Publisher—E. & H.T. Anthony, NYC

INDIAN ENCAMPMENT, SHOOTING GALLERY
Photographer—Hall Bros., Brooklyn

These three pictures show vendor huts, market booths and amusements set up in Saratoga's Indian Encampment during the late 1860s and early 1870s. This encampment, sometimes referred to as the Gypsy Camp or the Indian Camp and Park, was located near Congress Park on land bounded by Circular, Spring and Congress Streets.

Throughout most of the nineteenth century, such colorful camps were set up during the summer months in Saratoga. In earlier days, Indians were said to camp in the Pine Grove, near North Broadway. Later, in the 1850s, a large amusement site was located just off South Broadway where Ballston Avenue begins. In late Victorian times, that encampment moved two blocks south along the avenue. But during the post-Civil War Victorian years, the site pictured here near Congress Park was the largest. At the popular location, brisk trade in tourist items was carried on during the summer months. Curious native crafts, trinkets, souvenir glasses, pictures, and the like, were hawked to a crowd anxious to have fun and to take something home from Saratoga. The target shoot illustrated here was one of a number of amusements and games offered. Taintor's guidebook of 1882 describes the scene:

"A number of shanties, half tent, half hut are planted here, and a gypsy band, part Canadian, part Indian, live therein, and such sell things as good Indians are supposed to wear and use. Small boys urge the visitor to set up the persuasive cent, that they may hit it with their little arrows, and pocket the same. The performance is varied by sundry domestic scenes, with appropriate dresses and motions, and the whole affair is very picturesque, and is highly instructive to the inquiring mind. To be sure, it is a little theatrical, and one has grave doubts concerning the fidelity of the display of nature; but it serves to fill an idle hour, and amuse children and others."[14]

CAMP GREENMAN, UCC TENT SCENE

CAMP GREENMAN, UCC BAND MEMBERS

CAMP GREENMAN, UCC IN FORMATION AT THE CLARENDON HOTEL GARDEN

Photographer—D. Barnum, Boston and Saratoga

Saratoga Springs was an ideal place for holding conventions during the nineteenth century, as it had everything a convention organizer hoped for. The availability of hotel rooms and open space, along with an array of services and entertainment, prompted many to chose Saratoga as their place to meet. In 1869, the Utica Citizens Corp (UCC) held a camp meeting here and set up headquarters, known as Camp Greenman, on vacant grounds just south of the village beyond Greenridge Cemetery. The UCC was a militia group which included many Civil War veterans from New York's central Mohawk Valley. The three views pictured are from a large number of photographs Barnum took of the UCC that summer. Doubtless, many of those photos were taken just for the participants, but Barnum distributed a number of them commercially to a wider trade. Although the group marched and maneuvered at Camp Greenman, most of their members and families boarded in more luxurious surroundings at the Clarendon Hotel.

TOWN HALL AND COMMERCIAL BLOCK

Photographers—Hall Brothers, Brooklyn, NY

As the village grew and prospered after the Civil War, officials recognized a need to erect a large building to house its governmental offices. In 1871, the new Town Hall was completed and was capped by a grand bell tower with clock. Cast-iron lions guarded its main entrance on Broadway. Activities such as the music convention (seen in another view) took place in the upper floor theater inside Town Hall. The venue was used frequently throughout the year and was a well-attended place of entertainment, especially in the winters.

Entertaining troupes, minstrel shows, magicians, historical lecturers, performing acts and political affairs were booked here. Sometimes as many as three or four events in a week were held. For a time after the building was erected, the village Y.M.C.A. was also located in the building.

In this view, standing beyond Town Hall is the tall steeple of the old Presbyterian Church on Broadway. The commercial building to the right was built in 1871 by S. & G.W. Ainsworth and housed several businesses catering to a year-round trade. Charles R. Brown pur-chased this large commercial block in the fall of 1876, after bouncing back from bankruptcy in 1873 and recovering from three devastating fires to his old stores and property. Brown's paralysis never slowed his energetic outlook on life, and by the time he purchased this block of nine storefronts, he had earned enough capital to pay cash for the Ainsworth property. By the time he died in 1882, he had sold off all but the two corner storefronts. Brown's daughter Florence married Frederic Menges, who for many years operated a drug store at the corner shop shown here.

MUSICAL CONVENTION

Photographers—Baker and Record, Saratoga

Not all cultural pursuits and social activities took place during those hot days of July and August. This scene taken in the dead of winter shows a large group enjoying the second annual Musical Convention held in the village from January 28-31, 1873. An outgrowth of local efforts to promote music appreciation, the concerts were conducted by Professor L. O. Emerson, and J.P. Cobb is the distinguished pianist. The successful conventions drew talented musicians from as far away as Boston, in addition to a large number of singers from the villages surrounding Saratoga.

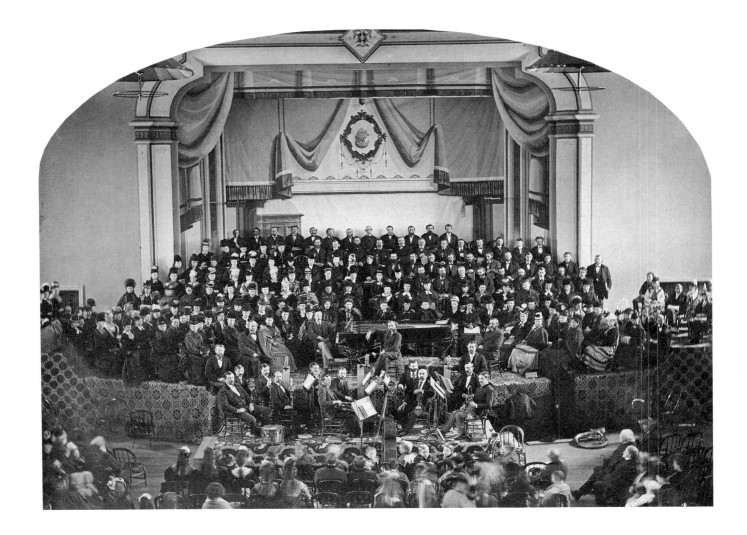

LOOKING NORTH, STORES AT THE OLD
AINSWORTH BLOCK

Photographer—D. Barnum, Boston and Saratoga

The street-level stores pictured here catered to affluent summer travelers during the Civil War period and offered visitors out for a stroll a fine selection of goods. This view looks northward up the old Ainsworth Block adjacent to the Union Hotel property. Prior to 1855, this site was occupied by Montgomery Hall, a hotel operated by Carey Moon.

EMMA HILL AND FRIENDS

Photographer—unknown Saratoga tintypist

On August 18, 1886, Emma Hill (center) and her friends sat in front of a painted studio backdrop and had this photograph taken. Sadie Mitchell, N. Herrick, William Hill (Emma's brother), and David Lovemoney (seated with his top hat) accompany her. Miss Hill was born in Wilton on February 25, 1865 and witnessed the grand Victorian years in Saratoga. On Christmas Day, 1893, she married Mr. Lovemoney, and the newlyweds moved to Connecticut shortly thereafter. The move was tragically followed by a year-long struggle with tuberculosis, after which she passed away. Her body was returned to Saratoga by train and buried in a local cemetery.

WINTER SCENE IN FRONT OF GRAND UNION HOTEL
Photographer—E.A. Record, Saratoga

This scene of the sidewalk in front of the Grand Union Hotel shows the village during the slow months of winter. Note the woman far down the walk appearing to be dwarfed by the snowbanks. Across Broadway is Congress Hall, and just visible in the far distance is the Windsor Hotel. Saratogians survived many great winter storms over the years, but the infamous 1888 blizzard was its most memorable. That storm blanketed the Springs with over 50¨ of snow in March.

WINTER SCENE ON BROADWAY
Photographer—W. H. Baker, Saratoga

The exact date of this pleasant winter view is not known, but whenever it was, a great deal of snow had to be shoveled, laboriously by hand at that. This is Broadway, in front of the commercial buildings between Spring Street and Phila Street beyond. The sign above the second floor at the right, only partially visible here, indicates that it is the Congress Hall Ballroom building. The "et Office" is from the sign for the New York Central Railroad ticket office quartered here.

DRY GOODS/HARDWARE STORE

Photographer—unknown

A reflection in the store windows seen in this unidentified photograph provides a clue to its whereabouts. The store is located on Broadway, diagonally across from the United States Hotel whose reflection is clearly evident. The building, known as the Gardner Block, was erected in 1873. Three gentlemen, perhaps owners or employees, stand in front of a hardware store which offers Bissell sweepers, wash wringers, wash boards, coal hods, and flat irons. Stores of this type were year-round establishments catering primarily to residents.

C.R. BROWN, JEWELER OPTICIAN STOREFRONT
Photographer—unknown

This late-1860s close-up shows Victorian silverplate, clocks, castor sets, watches, jewelry and opera glasses offered for sale by C.R. Brown at his No. 71 Broadway shop. This was Brown's streetside store in the Park Place Block he owned at the time. When this building burned to the ground in the fall of 1871, Brown narrowly escaped with his life. Rescuers pulled him from the raging inferno. The day after the fire, the *Daily Saratogian* reported that the store was a total loss except for one jewelry case. Brown never saw any of this valuable stock, however, since looters jumped in and made off with the contents of the case. Note at the left, a small sign reading "Bedortha" belonged to Dr. Bedortha, who operated his Saratoga Water Cure in Brown's building.

BROWN & AVERY,

Wholesale and Retail Dealers and

MANUFACTURERS OF CIGARS!

FROM

Foreign & Domestic Leaf,

No. 173 BROADWAY,

SARATOGA SPRINGS, N. Y.

All kinds of Tobacco and Smokers' Goods on Hand.

F. JOHNSON
Photographers—Warriner and Baker, Saratoga

A young-looking craftsman, identified as F. Johnson, poses with the products of his hard work. Exactly where he carried on his trade in Saratoga is not known, but judging from the miniature sleigh, he was an accomplished artisan.

WILLIAM H. CORBIN'S GROCERY STORE

Photographer—unknown

This small grocery store was located on Caroline Street in a large commercial building known as the Kearney Block. Located between Pavilion Place and Henry Street, the store was opened in the late 1880s by William Corbin, believed to be the gentleman standing in the doorway. Note that the awning rolled up in front of Corbin's business has "Saratoga Chips" imprinted upon it. Baskets of potatoes out front suggest that Corbin may have fried the potato chips fresh inside his store. Other baskets set along the sidewalk appear to offer onions, tomatoes, peanuts and other vegetables. Inside the shop window at the right, barely visible, is a poster which advertises the Saratoga-to-New York "Citizen's Line". In the 1880s, this popular route included steamship passage between New York City and Troy, combined with a train ride connecting Troy and Saratoga.

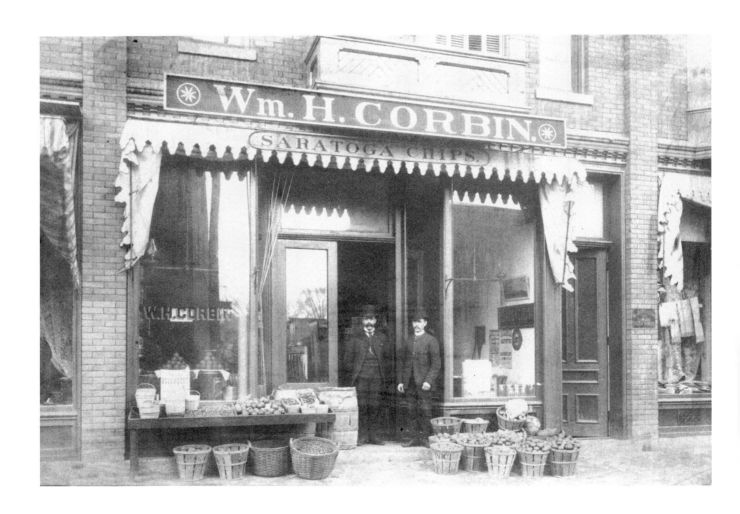

DRS. STRONG'S REMEDIAL INSTITUTE
Photographers—Baker and Record, Saratoga

Doctors S.S. and S.E. Strong operated this year-round house on Circular Street between Spring and Phila. Established as a place to "take the cure" in 1855, it was a refuge for people suffering a variety of medical maladies. Guests/patients and their families received the latest and most beneficial medical and mineral water treatments. An ad for the Institute from 1882 praised its "complete and elegant bath department affording the only Turkish, Russian, Roman and Electro-thermal baths in Saratoga."[15] The Strongs also provided musical entertainment, parlor lectures and lawn games, adding to the comfort and relaxation of guests.

PORCH SCENE, DRS. STRONG'S REMEDIAL INSTITUTE
Photographer—Saratoga Photograph Company, Saratoga

This mid 1870s closeup shows a well-dressed group of guests on the front porch of Strong's Institute. During the summer, the Institute was operated primarily as a boarding house, accepting a mostly transient clientele. For the rest of year, it took in more long-term boarders, most seeking the healthier life promised by its medicinal regime. Many wealthy and famous guests preferred this house, and the Institute carefully pointed this out to prospective boarders in its advertising. The decorative ironwork seen in the lower right of the picture is a carriage step, necessary since coaches were usually high off the ground and difficult to step out of.

RESIDENCE OF CHARLES S. LESTER
Photographers—Baker and Record, Saratoga

This substantial-looking Victorian house on North Broadway was the home of Judge Charles Lester, shown here standing next to the gate entrance. The 22-room residence was built in 1875 at a cost reported in the local press to be $30,000. Two carriage barns and a cottage on the property added another $4,400 to the expense. This is believed to be the most expensive private dwelling built in Saratoga that year, at a time when many smaller, handsome Victorian homes were built at a cost ranging from $1,500 to $5,000. Lester settled in Saratoga in the 1840s and practiced law for many years. In 1870, he was elected county judge, and was well-known for many years of civic and private service in the village and county. Devoting much of his time to these civic responsibilities, he gave willingly and often, chairing the Sunday school program at his church, for instance, or serving as president of the day for festivities marking the 100th anniversary of General Burgoyne's surrender at the Battle of Saratoga. Lester gave the opening speech to an enormous crowd of 40,000 assembled in the village of Schuylerville to mark the latter event and lay the cornerstone of the great stone obelisk commemorating the American victory.

RESIDENCE ON CIRCULAR STREET
Publisher—E. & H.T. Anthony, NYC

A young girl sits on a stone block carriage step in front of this charming Italianate-style house located on Circular Street across from Congress Park. The 1860s and 70s saw unprecedented growth in the village, and the construction boom brought many new public and commercial buildings and pleasant residential homes to the streets of Saratoga. The following note from the April 29, 1872, issue of the *Daily Saratogian* speaks to the construction in process: "as a note of the activity of building this spring in Saratoga, we are informed that at this time there are 56 residences in the course of construction within the village limits and this does not include the barns and outhouses."[16]

TEMPLE GROVE SEMINARY
Photographer—Saratoga Photograph Company, Saratoga

Located on Circular at the Spring Street intersection, Temple Grove was built by the Rev. Dr. Beecher in 1856. It served as a seminary institute for girls, but later came to be used as a summer hotel as well. In 1868, Dr. Charles Dowd purchased the building, expanded it, and added the observation tower. Dowd operated Temple Grove as a fashionable school for young women, but he is best remembered as the "inventor" of Standard Time. He advocated dividing the nation into time zones in order to bring standardization to the system. Dowd saw the adoption of his plans in 1883 when the country began using "National Time."

NEW YORK STATE PAVILION

Photographers—Centennial Photograph Co., Philadelphia, PA

In November, 1875, local architects Croff and Camp were selected from competition to design a magnificent residence worthy of national recognition. David Main, a local builder, was selected to construct the Saratoga creation, and during December he had a large crew of craftsmen and laborers working on the project. But this wonderful structure was not destined for the Springs,

and during the second week of January, 1876, all the building's component parts were carted off and began a long journey south from Saratoga to Philadelphia. A local construction crew accompanied the parts and pieces already assembled, along with a load of other building materials needed to complete their work. When they arrived in Philadelphia, the Saratoga workers began the task of assembling the building. By the end of March, it was pronounced the most substantial and the handsomest of all the

buildings in the area. During that summer, it would be seen by over one million citizens of the country, since the "Saratoga project" was, in fact, representing the great state of New York. This was the New York Pavilion, and sat prominently upon the grounds of the nation's Centennial Celebration here in Philadelphia. During that year, many Saratogians ventured to the celebration and were proud of the contribution of their community.

GLEN MITCHELL HOTEL

Photographer—W.H. Sipperly, Mechanicville, NY

The grounds of Glen Mitchell played host to many outdoor activities in the 1870s and early 1880s. Located just north of the village, the main house was erected by brothers George and Caleb Mitchell. Interestingly, in this view, upon the walls of the porch hang many portraits, though it is not known why they are here or whom they represent. The portraits could well belong to one of the numerous groups that frequently camped on the property. Glen Mitchell was often used by militia regiments for encampments, and baseball matches and foot races between visiting colleges and organizations were held here regularly. A driving park/trotting track was established on the grounds, as were buildings maintained by the Saratoga County Agricultural Society for their annual fairs. The spot was popular throughout the year, with the trotting races and sleigh races being well-attended regular events.

TOBOGGAN SLIDE, GLEN MITCHELL HOTEL

Photographer—T.J. Arnold, Ballston Spa, NY

Winter fun at the Glen Mitchell grounds also included a 2,000-foot toboggan slide erected on the property in December 1884 after the Saratoga Agricultural Society vacated the property and moved its annual fair to Ballston Spa. Great speed could be achieved on this long iced toboggan run, and three boys stand proudly and smile for the photographer, having accomplished the trip safely. The buildings in the background are from the days of the agricultural fairs. When the Glen Mitchell Hotel ceased operation, the property was taken over in 1886 by the Redemptorist Mission Fathers, who operated a school and mission house for many years at the location.

GENERAL U.S. GRANT AND FAMILY AT MT. MCGREGOR
Photographer—unknown

Ulysses S. Grant made trips to Saratoga Springs as a conquering hero and as the nation's president, and wonderful receptions were given in his honor. Late in life, Grant was diagnosed with throat cancer and returned for one final visit in the summer of 1885. Having almost no money to his name, Grant sought a place to spend the last days of his life, to finish writing his memoirs, and to earn enough money to provide for his family's well-being when he passed on. His fondness for the Saratoga region, and a generous offer from Joseph Drexel to use a cottage Drexel owned on Mt. McGregor, brought Grant here again. When he arrived, Grant continued the monumental task of finishing his manuscript. During that period, Grant was visited a number of times by his publisher, Mark Twain. Twain enjoyed Saratoga, too, and was seen on a number of occasions playing billiards in the village. The entire country mourned, when on July 23, 1885, the great General died, but he had finished his record for posterity. This view of Grant and family was taken on June 19, 1885, on the front porch of Drexel's cottage.

PRESIDENT GRANT'S BODY, TRANSFER BETWEEN TRAINS

GRANT'S FUNERAL TRAIN
Photographer—W.H. Baker, Saratoga (both views)

General Grant's body was brought off Mt. McGregor on the small narrow-gauge train pictured on the left. He was then transferred to the funeral train shown on the right. On the north side of Saratoga, these two railroad lines ran alongside each other, and it was there that this large crowd gathered to pay respects to the General. Note that many in the gathering wear ribbons and badges of the G.A.R. (Grand Army of the Republic, the north's Civil War veteran's organization), while still others have donned the uniforms worn in service decades earlier. Saratoga photographer W. H. Baker was on hand and took a series of views that day, including the closeup view of the train which eventually carried Grant to New York City, where he was laid to rest on a picturesque bluff over-looking the Hudson River. The little cottage on Mt. McGregor became known as Grant's Cottage. For years afterward, Civil War veterans, paying their respects, came to the small moun-taintop cottage to see where their beloved general had passed away. In the fall of 1889, the popularity of the cottage prompt-ed the State of New York to take it over, and Oliver P. Clark was appointed caretaker. For 27 years he cared for and maintained the setting. Clark, a Civil War veteran from the Utica area, had served in the 94th Infantry. His service to the Union had been long and noteworthy, and Grant and the little cottage on Mt. McGregor could have no better friend than O. P. Clark.

HOTEL BALMORAL, MT. MCGREGOR
Photographer—W.H. Baker, Saratoga

Just to the north of the village, the Palmertown Range of the Adirondacks rise abruptly near the hamlet of Wilton. This high spot has come to be known as Mt. McGregor. Recognizing the location as an ideal spot for a Victorian mountaintop hotel, Duncan McGregor purchased the property, cut a road through the woods and rocks, and built the Balmoral Hotel. Saratoga was nearby and provided ample crowds from which to draw visitors.

Advertising the mountain's charms and clean healthy air, the mountain resort was said to be "a thousand-acre mountain, ten miles north of and 1000 feet above Saratoga. Hay fever and asthma unknown at Mt. McGregor."[17] The lovely setting became a favorite day trip from Saratoga and was made easily accessible when the Saratoga and Mt. McGregor rail line was laid in the spring of 1882. In later years, more guests were lured to the mountain to visit Grant's Cottage, located only a few hundred yards away from the hotel. The hotel was visited by President Harrison and his vice president on August 20, 1891, when a country dinner was served to the them and about 100 invited guests. The Balmoral's life, however, was short, as it burned to the ground in December, 1897.

FIRST METHODIST EPISCOPAL CHURCH
Photographers—Baker and Record, Saratoga

Itinerant preachers traveling the muddy roads of Saratoga County brought Methodism to county residents and summer guests in the early 1800s. As church membership grew, the Methodist Episcopal Society was formed, and they occupied their first house of worship in 1830. In 1841, they occupied a new church on this Washington Street property purchased from Dr. John Clarke of Congress Spring fame. The edifice pictured was dedicated in 1871 and testifies to the continued growth of the Methodists. The tall mansard roof in the background sits atop a rear wing of the United States Hotel.

HOLLY WATERWORKS

Photographer—Wm. Sipperly, Mechanicville, NY

Water for village residents, businesses and hotels was provided by various sources and supplies developed during the nineteenth century. But the private wells and small reservoirs on the outskirts of the village, with pipes laid into town, were hard-pressed to keep up with demand. In the post-Civil War years, village leaders developed a plan to bring the abundant resources of Loughberry Lake to all of Saratoga. In 1871, the Holly engines and pumps seen in this view began supplying water throughout the village. The man sitting by the apparatus is most likely an employee of the waterworks.

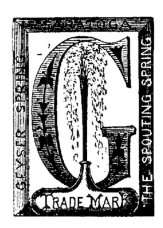

BROOK IN GEYSER PARK

Photographers—Baker and Record, Saratoga

Young boys play at streamside just below Geyser Falls in this scene from the mid-1870s. The Geyser Spring and bottling house is just out of view to the left. Trails wound their way around the various springs found here, and afforded a pleasant walk for the many visitors who came to enjoy the water. A few residences, a small hotel, a grist mill, and a train stop were just a short walk away.

TRAIN STOP AT EMPIRE SPRING
Photographers—McDonnald and Sterry, Saratoga

In 1881, a new rail line was laid from the village, beginning in the spring valley at Lake Avenue. This line headed towards High Rock and the Valley of the Ten Springs, passing close by Excelsior and Eureka springs. From there, the line headed east, eventually arriving at Saratoga Lake. By the following year, a line branched off and headed to Schuylerville and connections to New England. Along the line there were small whistle stops where passengers could board or leave the trains. The stop pictured here is the very first one after leaving the Lake Avenue depot. It was built near the High Rock and Star springs, which are just out of the view at the left. Barely visible in the background behind the station is the Empire Spring and bottling house.

MORRISSEY'S CLUB HOUSE
Photographers—Baker and Record, Saratoga

There was gambling in Saratoga prior to the Civil War, even though it was illegal. But John Morrissey took it to a much more organized, and even respectable, level when he arrived upon the scene in the early 1860s. Morrissey, a champion prize fighter, gambler and politician, raised in Troy, secured his fortune in the gambling business. Establishing gaming houses in New York City, he was soon drawn by the crowds and wealth at Saratoga, where he initially operated a gaming place on Matilda Street (Woodlawn Avenue). Morrissey eventually sought a better location for his business and bought property near Congress Spring, where this fine brick building was erected in 1870. Handsomely-appointed with Victorian furnishings, Morrissey's "Club House" was an instant success. Over the years, however, Morrissey's success was occasionally tempered by the cry of reform-minded residents and tourists alike who would have nothing to do with gambling. The following, somewhat cynical, description was given for potential visitors in the 1871 edition of Colt's *Tourist Guide Through the Empire State*:

As the Press of the country has teemed with accounts of the splendors of Morrissey's Club House in Saratoga, we wish to correct some of the false impressions which are afloat concerning it. We copy and present below a reliable statement of this establishment, from the pen of Mr. R.F. Dearborn, the admirable Saratoga Correspondent of OUR SOCIETY and other publications.

Few are the journals of city and country, says Mr. Dearborn, that have not contained some notice on account of Morrissey's Club House. It has become one of the first objects to which the attention of visitors is attracted. A very exaggerated idea of its magnificence has been excited by so much talk and the glowing accounts in the penny-a-liners. For instance, we are told that one of the "very finest" oil paintings in the country adorned its walls; but when we came to investigate, we learned that the expense of this "magnificent work of art" amounted to about three thousand five hundred dollars. We concluded that either Mr. M was exceedingly shrewd in purchasing, or else the finest paintings were at a discount.

The building is very substantial, and well furnished. That its furnishings are superior or equal to the first-class residences of our cities, is by no means true. During the past winter a large addition has been made to it, the main object of which, it is said, is for the selling of pools for the races. This is by far the finest part of the building.

The case of the Young Men's Christian Association vs. Morrissey remains yet undecided, but that association closed three other establishments for the same purpose. During the winter and spring, such efforts have been made by the leading citizens to restrain, within proper bounds, the vices and crimes incident to any fashionable resort, that it may be hoped that Saratoga will become the most moral, as it is now the most celebrated watering place in the world. Large numbers of the most highly cultivated, as well as the most wealthy people are among the summer residents of Saratoga, and the majority of its citizens will sustain this action for the suppression of open vice.[18]

Despite the effort, the Club House remained open throughout the Victorian years. Morrissey did not allow women to gamble, and he also kept local citizens away from the gaming tables. That, along with occasional generous gifts to local charities and politicians, helped keep the place open. Morrissey passed away in May, 1878. In the 1890s, Richard Canfield, another well-known gambler, took over the property and made many improvements to the house and grounds.

MORRISSEY'S POOL ROOMS
Photographer—unknown

Striped awnings hide not only the sun but what some believed were the shady dealings which took place inside. The homey structure on the old Putnam Street was another Morrissey property, and a walkway connected it to his more well-known Club House a few yards away. Morrissey drew an affluent clientele to this place, anxious for the action inside. Here, patrons wagered on horses running at Morrissey's track. An 1884 map identifies the building as the Saratoga Racing Association Rooms.

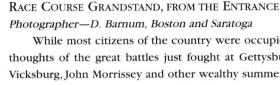

RACE COURSE GRANDSTAND, FROM THE ENTRANCE
Photographer—D. Barnum, Boston and Saratoga

While most citizens of the country were occupied with thoughts of the great battles just fought at Gettysburg and Vicksburg, John Morrissey and other wealthy summer guests were busy planning for a thoroughbred horse racing meet for Saratoga. That summer of 1863 saw a four-day meet, run on a Union Avenue track leased by Morrissey and used for trotting races since 1847. The success of the meet led to the immediate formation of the Saratoga Racing Association which purchased land across the street. On that large parcel, they planned a larger course to provide facilities capable of handling the expected crowds. By the summer of '64, a new track, called the Saratoga Race Course, was ready. This view from the late 1860s, by Barnum, shows the original grandstand of the new course. Barnum, always with an eye and camera for catching events, was one of the apparently few photo artists who took and distributed views of the race course in those earliest days. Interestingly, although the track drew large crowds, it seems to have received little attention from photographers and publishers of tourist guide books during that early period. *Taintor's Guidebook,* a standard tourist reference in its day, devoted only a little more than a paragraph to horse racing in over 100 pages of information about the Saratoga region. Nonetheless, even without that publicity, the entire world was well aware of this important Saratoga attraction. Major newspapers across the country covered the action.

ENTRANCE TO THE RACE TRACK
Photographer—D. Barnum, Boston and Saratoga

The main entrance gate to the Race Course was on Union Avenue, shown in this view from the late 1860s. Beyond the handsome entrance is the back side of the grandstand. From early views of the track, it is apparent that men, including young boys, dominated the crowds. Comparatively few women are seen in the early photos, although newspaper accounts during the period would lead one to conclude there were scores of fashionable women all about. While African-American jockeys and horse trainers were active participants at the course, African-Americans were officially barred as racetrack patrons at this time.

HURDLE RACE, SARATOGA RACE COURSE
Photographer—D. Barnum, Boston and Saratoga

The Race Course has been readied for a hurdle race in this early view. The jump appears to consist of tree boughs and branches propped up along something strung across the track. The jumping races became quite popular, and by the 1870s it evolved into the steeplechase where horse and rider had to complete a longer course with obstacles like mud, water, hedge and brush along the way. Note the two judging stands on either side of the main track, and the track area which seems to angle off to the right. The early track included a diagonal section across the oval which was used as a starting point for some of the races. By the mid-1870s, the open-air stand was given a cover very similar to the main grandstand.

RACE COURSE, GETTING READY FOR THE START
Photographer—D. Barnum, Boston and Saratoga

This wonderful photograph by Barnum is another important historical record of the early track. The open-air bleacher section, probably the general admission of its day, was located down from the covered stand on the way to the first turn. Apparently, the horses are readying for a race in this picture, as all heads are turned toward the starting line. During the late 1860s, the Race Course offered six days of summer racing, but it increased to twelve, and then to fourteen days during most of the 1870s. A dramatic increase occurred in 1877, when it held 27 days of racing. Growing ever more popular, it later averaged around 30 days of summer racing for the remainder of the Victorian years.

DARTMOUTH CREW
Photographers—Baker and Record, Saratoga

In the mid-1870s, the Saratoga region was very fortunate to play host to important intercollegiate regattas whose participants rowed a three-mile course across Saratoga Lake. This photograph shows the crew from Dartmouth College standing by their boathouse located on the east side of the lake just south of Cedar Bluff. The national event, which drew schools like Cornell, Harvard, Columbia, and Yale, was described for readers across the country by a large contingent of press covering the events.

DARTMOUTH BOAT, TOWN HALL
Photographers—Baker and Record, Saratoga

Festivities associated with the regatta took place throughout the area. One such event was held here at the Town Hall theater where Dartmouth crew and fans attended a party complete with a mock sailboat christened "Dartmouth." Whether this affair was a post-event award ceremony, or just part of the many festivities, is uncertain. Likewise, it is unclear what all the small boxes stacked neatly on the boat were for. Speculation suggests that they were given to the race participants.

GRAND STAND, INTERCOLLEGIATE REGATTA, 1874

Photographers—Baker and Record, Saratoga

This large group was gathered at the northwestern end of Saratoga Lake to view the 1874 intercollegiate regatta. It represents a small portion of the huge crowds which assembled all around the lake for the event. Here, in front of the spectators, uniformed musicians entertained the throngs. Considerable planning, preparation and construction went into preparing the site. This grandstand was located lakeside in front of publisher Frank Leslie's property, where the race ended that year. The three-mile course was moved south of the Leslie property by 1876, ending at a new grandstand at Ramsdill's Point. Unfortunately, the intercollegiate event was suspended after 1876. While other regattas continued on the lake in the 1880s and '90s, attracting large audiences, they did not have the stature of the national intercollegiate events.

REPORTERS AND COLLEGE STAND AT THE 1874 INTERCOLLEGIATE REGATTA

Photographers—Baker and Record, Saratoga

Beyond the general grandstand was an area for college representatives and reporters covering the event. (Note the poles with flags flying atop for the schools participating in the regatta.) Two barge-like boats in the foreground carry many men, and the one on the left had a table-like counter on it which served as a writing surface for reporters. The cottage in the background was part of the extensive holdings of publisher Frank Leslie who summered in Saratoga on property he called Interlaken.

FRANK LESLIE'S RESIDENCE, SARATOGA LAKE
Photographer—unknown

Built with Adirondack rustic-style porches, the residence of Mr. Leslie clings to the hillside on the northwest edge of Saratoga Lake. Leslie became wealthy from publishing his popular newspaper, *Leslies' Weekly*. In the 1860s and '70s his chief competitor in the national marketplace was *Harper's Weekly*. The many acres of Leslie's Interlaken property, laid out in 1873, appeared park-like, and contained Adirondack stick-style accessories, from benches to covered gazebos. Leslie spent a fortune creating the walks and carriage roads, planting trees and greenery, and embellishing the grounds with an interesting assortment of features. During the summer, he opened the grounds to the public.

E. R. STEVENS, Jr.,

BOOKSELLER AND STATIONER,

CALIFORNIA CEDAR, F. LESLIE PROPERTY.
Photographers—Baker and Record, Saratoga

Among the whimsical excesses of the Victorian era, this event of June 1874 stands out. A giant, centuries-old California cedar tree trunk was cut into sections and shipped to Saratoga to rise again here at Leslie's Interlaken. The workmen have paused briefly from their duties assembling and covering the 28-feet-in-diameter trunk which, when completed, would be yet another rustic decoration for the grounds. When finished, the shelter was surrounded by a fence, and its multi-level roof was topped by a star fashioned from sticks. The house and grounds of the Leslie property were put up for sale after his death in 1880.

BRIGGS HOUSE, SARATOGA LAKE
Photographers—Baker and Record, Saratoga

The Briggs House was a good starting point for exploring the area around Saratoga Lake. The small hotel was the product of local real estate agent and broker John P. Conkling who was probably more responsible than any other person for developing and popularizing the lake area in the 1870s. Conkling owned a number of pleasure boats at the lake in the early '70s and purchased the partially-developed White Sulphur Springs property to provide a destination for the boats on the lake's southern end. With that place developed into a first-class resort, he purchased vacant property from Mr. J. Briggs on the north side of the lake and built this hotel to serve as starting point for his steamers. His well-known boats, including the Commodore Brady and Una, made hourly crossings between the two hotels, pulling drawing-room barges in tow during the summer season.

Conkling also turned his attention to the crude road on the east side of the lake. At his own expense, he developed it into a fine driving surface for carriages, covering the three miles from the bridge to his White Sulphur property. He opened a stage line from Saratoga to his lakeside destinations and advertised widely, which increased patronage all around the lake.

Another convenience Conkling provided was especially appreciated by visiting businessmen and reporters attending the lake regattas: telegraph lines connecting his two hotels with Saratoga and with the Atlantic and Pacific Telegraph network. This allowed instant communication with the rest of the country.

In this view, beyond the Briggs House to the right was Moon's Lake House, while to the left, travelers could pass over the bridge crossing the lake's outlet, and then down the long pleasant road along the lake's eastern side. In 1881, when the Saratoga Lake Railway opened, rail passengers from the village ended their train ride at the Briggs where a large new steamboat, *Lady of the Lake*, was ready to take them on an excursion. The *Lady of the Lake* was a huge iron boat with three decks, and capable of carrying hundreds of passengers.

LAKESIDE AT THE BRIGGS
Photographer—unknown

Framework covers this boat under construction along the shores of Saratoga Lake. Some workmen posed for the photographer, while others continued their duties building the small steam-powered vessel which would one day ferry tourists upon the lake. The Briggs Hotel is in the background in this photo from 1876. In December of that year, the manager of the Briggs, Mr. Cook, inaugurated an ice track for trotting horses out in front of the hotel. His first race on the straight line track was held on December 27 over the frozen lake. The local press reported that 800-1,000 spectators came to see the main event, a $600 match race, and that there was active pooling among the crowd.

MOON'S LAKE HOUSE
Publisher—E. & H.T. Anthony, NYC

One of the best-known destinations on the lake at this time was Moon's Lake House. A bountiful table was always set at this fine restaurant, frequently attended by some of the richest and most influential of Saratoga's guests. Carriage passengers were let off at this porch on the side of Moon's, and tables were set for guests inside, as well as on the grounds on the other side of the building. This picture dates from the summer of 1865. Moon's is best remembered as the place where the "Saratoga Chip" was invented, which is how, for many years, the little slices of American cuisine were known across the country. Over time, they lost their geographic affiliation and came to be popularly called by their generic name—potato chips.

MOON'S LAKE HOUSE, FROM THE FRONT
Photographer—Sterry, Saratoga

Bottles of wine, champagne and glasses have been neatly placed on each of the tables in this scene. In all likelihood, the photographer has set up the picture with the owner's assistance. Note each wine bottle's label neatly points toward the photographer. The view was probably taken during a slow time of day, as it may otherwise have been difficult for the photographer to keep the patrons still long enough for a photo. Paths to the right led down the hill to the lake, where Moon operated a billiard hall in a small frame building, along with a shooting gallery outside.

VIEW ON SARATOGA LAKE
Photographer—D. Barnum, Boston and Saratoga

This scenic photograph shows passengers aboard a sailboat and a steamboat at Moon's Lake House dock. Looking beyond, in a north-easterly direction, is the toll bridge built across the lake where it narrows to form the Fish Creek outlet.

HENRY MOON'S LAKE SIDE HOUSE
Photographers—McDonnald and Sterry, Saratoga

Henry S. Moon had been a captain on one of the steamers sailing from Carey Moon's Lake House until 1872, when he apparently decided to run his own place. Henry took over a nearby establishment operated for many years as Capt. Abel's Lake Side. In order to draw customers from his father's well-known place, Henry had the huge sign, shown here, painted across his carriage building. This small but popular place advertised game and fish dinners, as well as boats and bait for fishing. Judging from the garments, it appears that the two men sitting at the left are regatta participants.

CEDAR BLUFF HOTEL FROM DAISY HILL
Photographers—Baker and Record, Saratoga

An unidentified man stands in a field of daisies and gazes down the hill toward the Cedar Bluff Hotel. This small hotel was one of many pleasant hostelries around the lake offering a room with meals of fresh farm produce, fish and game. The eastern slopes of the lake region were home to many productive farms. In this pleasant scene from the mid-1870s, rail fences enclose the fields. Good times for Cedar Bluff ended when, after the death of the owner, the hotel fell on hard times and was destroyed by fire on September 11, 1883.

WHITE SULPHUR SPRINGS HOTEL

Photographers—Baker and Record, Saratoga

A small group stands on the dock at the White Sulphur Springs Hotel, probably waiting for a ride upon the lake. Located south of Snake Hill, the hotel was one of the largest establishments on the lake at the time. The lovely place seen here is primarily the product of John Conkling, who purchased the property in 1874 and fully developed it into a first-class Victorian resort. The facility was leased and operated by Simeon Leland and Co. An elegant bathhouse on the grounds offered both plain and mineral baths. Guests arrived by coach, following the road around the lake, or were ferried by boat across the water. The property around the hotel, almost 200 acres, was covered with miles of walkways and cool restful places to stop and relax. Huge old-growth pine and hardwood trees were said to be plentiful along these paths. The hotel took its name from a nearby sulphur spring claiming to be the clearest sulphur water in the world. Probably no detailed scientific study ever actually proved this claim, but it did sound good when advertising the hotel.

WHITE SULPHUR SPRING, SARATOGA LAKE
Photographer—H. Brown, Saratoga

A dipper boy in the pit serves up refreshment to patrons at the White Sulphur Spring. The Saratoga area had many spring pavilions, but this is believed to be the only one built in the Adirondack rustic style.

PIAZZA, WHITE SULPHUR SPRINGS HOTEL
Photographers—Baker and Record, Saratoga

An aproned waiter, momentarily detained from his duties by the camera, stands proudly alongside the well-dressed group on the White Sulphur Springs Hotel piazza. Such handsome scenes epitomize the Victorian summer life in Saratoga.

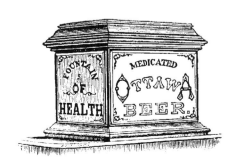

CHAPTER 8
THE 1890'S—END OF AN ERA

As the 1890s began, Saratoga exhibited many marvelous examples of its own prosperity. Everywhere, the features of a very successful Victorian resort were boldly proclaimed. Saratoga could look back with pride on many important gatherings, conventions and sporting events of the past. A new day was at hand, and the '90s would prove to be yet another period of great change and transition. Saratoga would continue to be the scene of excitement, with conventions, summer parties and parades, but it would also be a community facing an uncertain future, wrestling with social questions and important concerns about its character. The times would be filled with controversy over gambling. Saratoga had become America's center for summertime gambling, to the delight of some and the dismay of others. Like other communities across the nation, the village would also grapple with changes brought on by technology and industry. With the 20th century rapidly approaching, vast change was on the horizon. All around, there were obvious indications.

Construction had changed significantly, compared to the great boom years of the 1870s. The building of colossal hotels and expansive commercial blocks was a pursuit of times gone by, although work crews still busied themselves with residences and smaller commercial properties. Especially noticeable now were the many wonderful summer cottages being built by families who had previously boarded in the hotels. New entertainment and assembly spaces were constructed during the decade in an attempt to attract more year-round business to keep the hotels filled and the shops and restaurants busy.

Along Broadway, horse-drawn carriages and wagons still made their way up and down the tree-lined street. The stately landmark elms were a cherished asset of the community, but now there was an air of maturity about their summer greenery. In the 1890s, beautiful Broadway became less picturesque as modern technology infringed upon the scene. Tall utility poles placed along the street distributed power and carried communication through dozens of unsightly wires strung between glass insulators. Criss-crossing Broadway, they were

an ever-present reminder of a new era, and proved that technology could both enhance and detract from a community.

Bicycling had become a very popular form of everyday transportation and recreation in the Victorian years. Cyclists boldly dodged in and out between horse-drawn buggies and wagons. So many people had taken to riding that the village had to begin considering special bikeways to provide for their safety. While the bicycle provided a certain amount of speed, mobility and independence, many were excited by the promise of a new mode of transportation, dubbed the "horseless carriage," though few could ever imagine such contraptions taking the place of the horse and buggy. Electric trolleys were also becoming an important means of transportation during this time and began to take the place of the old horse and carriage trips out to Saratoga Lake, the Race Course and the Geysers. Trolleys seemed no more than short railroad lines, and so were embraced without the skepticism reserved for the horseless carriage.

Many residents and tourists still enjoyed the springs and baths, even though there were signs that the number of people devoted to the water was on the wane. The ritual morning pilgrimages were being replaced by private consumption from bottles and jugs. But while the clientele appeared to be dwindling at some springs, at a few popular springs the crowds were, in fact, growing. In the 1880s, spacious year-round drink halls had been built over Hathorn Spring and Patterson Spring on Phila Street, prompted by the popularity of the enclosed Victorian Congress arcade. Thousands visited the pleasant new halls, ostensibly to drink the water, but the spindle-back chairs, chestnut tables and wicker rockers also provided a wonderful opportunity for patrons to sit and visit. Friends and strangers would gather to chat and spend time, leisurely enjoying a social visit and an opportunity to see and be seen, a far cry from the more intimate tiny spring pavilions of a generation earlier. In these large drink halls, the mineral springs found their most successful adaptation to the new resort which Saratoga had become. Across from Patterson Spring on Phila, the elegant new Saratoga Baths provided every bath, water cure and immersion technique ever conceived. The large facility was said to be the finest bath-house in the entire country and enjoyed an active following.

A brand new venue for special events was established when Convention Hall was erected just south of Congress Park on Broadway. Completed in the fall of 1893, the public facility, with seating for 5000, allowed Saratoga to attract even larger conventions and events. Its particularly fine acoustics also made the hall an ideal setting for musical entertainment. The assemblies were big business for the village and many, like the State Republican convention in September, 1895, were widely publicized. Others were less known, such as when the "colored men of the state convene in Saratoga Springs and organize the Afro-American Republican Organization of the State of New York," held in August of that same year.[19]

Theater productions had long been favored entertainment at the Springs. Plays and operas were performed on open hotel lawns and in playhouses on and off Saratoga's Broadway. When the old Putnam Music Hall on Phila Street burned in 1896, the elegant Theater Saratoga quickly rose in its place. The Theater Saratoga seated an audience of 950 in a three-tiered interior and was said to be the finest house north of New York City. Summer travelers flocked to its offerings but, like the theater in Town Hall, it was also used frequently throughout the rest of the year.

The '90s also brought an expanding industrial base to Saratoga, something largely missing from the old resort setting where a service economy prevailed. The G. F. Harvey Company was incorporated in 1891, and became known across the nation for its highly-regarded medicine salve, Saratoga Ointment. The company had started out years before as a small local firm, but it gradually gained a national market for the pharmaceuticals it produced. Baker and Shevlin was outgrowing its small foundry and machine shop in the middle of the village, just off Broadway near Caroline and Putnam Street. The company would begin to look elsewhere for property and one day erect a huge new facility out on Ballston Avenue by the Congressville section of town. The company produced massive iron and bronze castings and tooled machines for shipment across the country. Carbonic gas companies also began their move into Saratoga during these years. Locating primarily on the south side of the village, they would build sprawling industrial sites to take advantage of a component found in Saratoga's waters. Viewed as welcomed employers initially, the effects of the gas companies' actions would eventually prove disastrous.

Two men of vast wealth worked on architectural landmarks in the '90s. While both would be admired for their construction projects, they stood on opposite sides of an important issue confronting the village. Gambler Richard Canfield placed himself in the public eye when he transformed John Morrissey's Club House into a more elegant gambling hall and enhanced its grounds. Canfield offered a refined and respectable venue for gambling, and many welcomed his approach. But Canfield's efforts were not universally appreciated. Some viewed his embellishment of the gambling club as little more than constructing a veil to hide the evil inside.

On the outskirts of the village was another wealthy Saratogian hard at work putting up a comfortable new home for his family. Wall Street financier Spencer Trask began the building in 1891, calling his palatial new residence "Yaddo." A colossal landmark of the new rich, the stone mansion rose on the spot where Trask's old home had been destroyed by fire earlier that year. Trask, a reformer, was against gambling and spent a small fortune trying to rid the village of the illegal activity. Some believed his efforts were self-serving and designed to make Saratoga a haven for the aristocratic super-rich, like Newport, Rhode Island.

Throughout the Victorian years, the thoroughbred horse-racing seasons had been very popular and well-publicized. Thousands attended the meets but, despite all the notoriety and press, there were many who viewed the racing season with indifference, never setting foot on the grounds. The debate over gambling and horse racing constantly festered within the community. The gambling houses were the reformist's primary target, but horse racing was also of great concern, and the races and gambling halls shared many of the same patrons.

The Saratoga Race Course had enjoyed a standing as "the" place for summer horse racing in the years following the Civil War. However, by the 1890s, Saratoga's success had long since encouraged the establishment of race tracks elsewhere. Horse breeders provided a growing supply of stock, and other tracks began to challenge Saratoga's standing and prestige. The facility also began to show its age after three decades of wear and tear.

In 1892, Gottfried Walbaum took over control of the aging race course, much to the chagrin and dismay of the old racing establishment. Many racing aristocrats viewed Walbaum as little more than a common gambler, "a bum from the Bowery." He was not one of them, not one of the "old guard." However, Walbaum's first order of business at Saratoga was bold and highly-regarded. He made significant improvements throughout the grounds, the most notable of which was a sorely-needed, beautiful new grandstand. He also readily opened his doors to African-Americans, something early track management would not do.

But some of Walbaum's other changes and business practices were not so well appreciated. Walbaum welcomed women and children to the track and provided them with their own betting ring. That action, along with a reputation for other notorious activities, brought the crusading reporter Nellie Bly to Saratoga in the summer of 1894 to investigate the scene. When she left, Bly told the rest of the world how she found pervasive scandal, fraud and disgrace at Saratoga. The good citizens of the country were outraged when she described in *The World* how young boys and girls, some no more than six years old, were betting at the track. Under her banner headline "OUR WICKEDEST SUMMER RESORT", Bly told of "Reputable and Disreputable Women, Solid Merchants, Bankers, Sports, Touts, Criminals, and Race-Track Riff-Raff Crazed by the Mania for Gold."[20]

In 1893, Caleb Mitchell had begun his term as village president, and he felt the sting of Bly's headlines personally. Mitchell, a Saratoga merchant and developer of the Glen Mitchell Hotel and park north of the village, was no ordinary politician. He owned a gambling hall right on Broadway across from the United States Hotel, a situation which caused considerable concern for many and added fuel to the controversy over gambling. Bly labeled him "'Cale' Mitchell, Village President and Boss Gambler".[21] The negative press gave reform-minded Saratogians a new ally in State Senator Edgar Truman Brackett. Legislation carefully crafted by Brackett in Albany led to Mitchell's ouster from office. The reformers gained the upper hand, and the gambling halls were shut down in 1895 and, in 1896, the Race Course lay idle for the season.

The reformers, however, enjoyed only a brief victory. Summer visitors were anxious to return to the faro tables and roulette wheels. Canfield was likewise anxious to reap a profit again from his Saratoga investment, as was Walbaum at the track. Many local residents also complained about the resulting economic loss, as they too sustained their livelihood either directly or indirectly from the gaming business. Well-placed "inducements" and enticing promises were all that were needed in the face of economic hardship. By the summer of 1897, a compromise had been reached and gambling, still just as illegal as ever, was allowed to resume. The track, Canfield's Club House, and five other gambling establishments were given "permission" to open (though none on Broadway opened again). Mitchell was still out of a job, and his gaming hall remained closed. Walbaum continued at the helm at the Race Course, but he stayed behind the scenes and avoided the public spotlight. The turmoil of the 1890s had tarnished the gilded track. Prominent racing families and their horses stayed away, and it seemed racing season would never again be the same.

Symbolic of the passing of an era and changing of the guard in the 1890s was the death of a number of aging Saratogians who had played an important part in the rise of the village. Once energetic young residents, they would now pass the torch to a new generation. Seymour Ainsworth, who was probably responsible for the construction of more buildings in Saratoga than any other single person, died in 1890. His ventures had spanned decades and included many storefronts and commercial blocks on Broadway. At one time or another he claimed part ownership in both Union Hall and the new United States Hotel. His interest in the springwater business included the High Rock and Favorite springs. He was widely admired for his part in developing High Rock Spring with its eagle-topped pavilion.

Merchant James H. Wright died in 1891 after many years operating a tailoring establishment on Broadway and serving in several public offices. A young Wright, and others like him, had been lured by the promise and vitality of Saratoga. With little fanfare they set about earning a respectable living, supporting both the summer and year-round trade, and helped make Saratoga the great success that it was.

In 1894, with the passing of Nathaniel Sylvester, the village and county lost a well-respected attorney and historian. He published his landmark *History of Saratoga County* in 1878, but was known for other works as well.

Dr. Robert Hamilton also passed away in 1894 after a long and distinguished career. The medical establishment and water cure he operated for decades along Congress Street near Broadway, and later on Franklin Street, offered hope and treatment for many residents and travelers. The Crescent Hotel and the Grand Central Hotel, in which he had part ownership, rose from ashes, testifying to his resilient nature and his continuing belief in Saratoga's future.

Carey Moon, popular host at his well-attended lakeside house and restaurant, died in 1895. His establishment was a frequent stop for many fun-loving, fashionable and wealthy guests who visited Saratoga, especially during the 1860s and '70s. His house would forever be immortalized as the birthplace of the potato chip.

In 1893, Franklin Smith, a former hardware store owner from Boston turned dreamer/community planner/social architect, began to raise concerns about the promotion and future direction of Saratoga. Smith was well acquainted with the village, having arrived in Saratoga a few years earlier to create on Broadway his much-heralded House of Pansa, a museum-like reproduction of a house destroyed in ancient Pompeii by the eruption of Mount Vesuvius in 79 AD. Many citizens listened intently to what he said about the need to work toward "A Greater Saratoga". Smith and others saw stagnation in the community and were concerned that with no organized plan to restore Saratoga's preeminence, the village would not prosper and grow, but be left to drift and degenerate into a resort of no particular note.

One problem Smith identified was the need to devise more attractive and refined entertainment. This was partly born of a personal distaste for gambling and horse racing, and the belief that such activity gave the village a bad reputation. Smith thought that, left unattended, gambling would destroy the village. He further believed Saratoga would benefit from an increase in cultural and intellectual activity which could be accomplished by attracting more religious, literary, social, medical and scientific gatherings. Beyond merely boarding new conventioneers, Smith thought the community might benefit by incorporating some of the culture of these conventioneers into the very fabric of their own lives. A refined, uplifted, educated collective consciousness would be the result.

To enhance Saratoga's economic fortunes, Smith believed the summer season needed to be extended to begin in May and run into October. He also thought more varied accommodations, including hotels offering more affordable summer rates, should be a priority for the community. Crucial to Smith's plans was an organized approach to advertising and promoting the village and all it had to offer. Smith also lamented the sorry condition of Saratoga's spring valley. In his opinion, spring valley and many of its shops and buildings had become little more than shanties and firetraps in need of condemnation. Certainly, this was no environment worthy of the "Queen of Spas."

A man of vision and foresight who thought in grand terms, Smith lobbied to create a great spa environment much like the famous watering places of Europe. He advocated ridding spring valley of all its unsightly buildings to create a great mineral spring park extending from Congress Park, through the valley past High Rock, down to Red Spring. Well-versed in the classic civilizations, Smith drew up park plans with a traditional, albeit over-ambitious, approach. His thoughts and ideas rang true to some Saratoga residents who viewed the opulent and flamboyant style of the Victorian era with distaste. They longed for a return to more time-honored and traditional architecture. While some thought Smith's schemes far-fetched, even ridiculous, many others were inspired by his visions. Most of his plans were never realized, but the issues he brought forth were real concerns and served as a wake-up call for Saratoga as it approached the 20th century.

The inauguration of Saratoga's floral fete and parades in 1894 was one outgrowth of Smith's proposals. Village residents energetically embraced his plans to showcase the good in the village and to extend the summer season to June and September. All Broadway, and much of the rest of the village, was colorfully decked out for the events. Saratogians paraded the streets draped in flowers, while carriages, wagons and bicyclists were laden with floral arrangements and greenery. Crowds came from afar to witness the colorful events. The Floral Parade and parties helped keep Saratoga in the spotlight, and the successful events enriched the culture and economy of the community. The first parade, held in September, 1894, was said to be attended by over 25,000 spectators, including 1000 who packed the front piazza of Congress Hall. In 1896, the popular annual event reportedly drew 100,000.

Despite all the good they brought, the Floral Festivals and Smith's other plans could not restore the bygone Victorian glory days of Saratoga, nor propel the village into a new age. An era was ending, and the world was changing in ways no one man, nor an entire community, could control. The age of the automobile was at hand, and it rang the death knell for this glorious time in Saratoga's history.

NEW GRANDSTAND AT SARATOGA RACE COURSE
Photographers—Epler and Arnold, Saratoga

When Gottfried Walbaum took over control of the Race Course in 1892, one of his first steps was to provide patrons with this beautiful new grandstand. The late-Victorian, Queen Anne-style facility was topped with a distinctive peaked roofline, and a fanciful new judges' stand was erected at the finish line. The racing meet had lost the shine and prestige it had enjoyed in previous decades, and doubtless Walbaum hoped the grandstand and a few other changes would restore the luster and provide for him a tidy profit. This view was taken shortly after Walbaum completed the renovations, and a relatively small gathering is apparently beginning to assemble for the day's races.

Walbaum's years at the helm, however, were marked by controversy. Throughout the period, the rumblings of the reform-minded, who never accepted gambling, were constantly heard, and they even managed to have the track shut down for one season. Many residents had become increasingly concerned about the negative image created in the press by gambling and racing. In 1894, an estimate of track attendance was taken to show its out-of-proportion notoriety, compared to the other things which made summers so special in Saratoga. While the accuracy of the numbers can be disputed, the sentiment rang true when it was stated, "The writer has investigated the attendance at the races and the highest number including employees and hangers on is 2,000. This number must include the gaming fraternity, for the gaming rooms are all deserted during the races. Where, then, are the 38,000 of the 40,000 which is the estimated number of people for the month of August, or at the time of the races."[22]

RACE TRACK AND JUDGE'S STAND, FROM THE NEW CLUB
HOUSE

Photographer—E. Doubleday, Saratoga

From inside the new grandstand, patrons sat in bent-
wood chairs and looked out at this picturesque scene. The
finish line is at the right, and the whimsical judges' stand at
trackside was appropriately topped by a horse and jockey
weathervane. There is little indication from the pleasant
scene that times were so troubling for the track.

ENTRANCE TO INDIAN CAMP

Photographer—G. Gould, Saratoga

A policeman walking his beat, and a group of visitors, obliged the photographer by posing for this 1890s view of Saratoga's Indian Encampment. At this time, there were actually two separate camps operated by A.F. Mitchell. One was still near Congress Park, but another camp was on Ballston Avenue, two blocks south of where it meets Broadway. Both had the festive atmosphere of small amusement parks, and for those inclined, there were all kinds of fun and thrills offered by various games of skill and chance. Attendants stood ever ready to pluck pocket change from tourists anxious to amuse them-

selves. Every manner of affordable Saratoga souvenir was offered from shacks and huts which many called home for the season. At the Ballston Avenue location, the most adventuresome visitors would hop aboard the Indian Encampment's exciting thrill ride, a roller coaster. A huge latticework of posts and timbers built along the avenue bordering the camp carried the thrill seekers. Others would take a trip on the old favorite, the circular railway, which had been moved here from its previous Congress Park location. Note in this view the large decorative sign hanging on the left advertising the camp's photo studio. Inside, tourists could sit for a quick photo, many examples of which hang out in front of the business.

FRONT OF GRAND UNION HOTEL

Photographer—F. Harwood, Schaghticoke, NY

Maturing elm trees in front of the Grand Union Hotel on Broadway have raised high their summer foliage, revealing more of the hotel's front than seen in summer photos of the previous decades. In the 1890s, the hotel continued its important place in the Saratoga season, still drawing a clientele which attracted attention. Horse-drawn coaches wait out in front of the hotel for their next jaunt.

SIDEWALK SCENE IN FRONT OF THE AMERICAN AND ADELPHI HOTELS

Photographer—F. Harwood, Schaghticoke, NY

Flowers and greenery deck this sidewalk scene in front of the American Hotel and, just beyond, the Adelphi Hotel on Broadway. The American was built of brick in 1840. The Adelphi was built during the slow season between 1876 and 1877. In this view, the village has been decorated for the much- anticipated Second Annual Floral Festival parade held in September, 1895. The parades were part of the well-orchestrated plans designed to showcase the good in Saratoga and extend its summer season. Note in this photograph evidence of the technological advances in photography and changes in fashion, compared to the 1860s. The instantaneous action of the young lad pulling up his sock and the swinging umbrella in the hands of the lovely woman have been captured with split-second timing.

STREET SCENE, LOOKING NORTH ON BROADWAY.
Photographer—F. Harwood, Schaghticoke, NY

In this scene, a banner strung across Broadway in front of the United States Hotel advertises "Second Annual Floral Fete, September 5th 1895." The parade and various other scheduled floral events brought large crowds who were treated to a visual spectacle the likes of which would be hard to imagine. The benefits were, arguably, most enjoyed by Saratoga's business community, which saw a flurry of activity in their shops. This scene appears quiet, probably taken a few days before the event. Passing coaches make their way along the village's main street which in the 1890s is still hard pack with cobble sides.

MASONS AT WORK IN SARATOGA
Photographer—unknown

Busy masons paused briefly from their duties to have this photograph taken during the mid-1890s. Alexander Martin, the third from the right, wearing the vest and tie, was a local contractor during the era, and, presumably, here his crew is working on a chimney for a new Saratoga residence. Compared to the early days of photography, shots of a personal nature like this became much more common after 1890.

WOMEN DRESSED IN ADVERTISING COSTUMES

Photographers—Epler and Arnold, Saratoga

Exactly why these young women are dressed in the wonderful costumes is not known. Speculation suggests the group might have been associated with the floral parades, or perhaps some trade fair in the 1890s. Why the gentleman, who appears out of place in the scene, is included is a mystery as well. The businesses represented in the colorful scene are primarily Saratoga concerns, but Troy, New York, is identified on a couple of them.

BICYCLISTS NEAR LINCOLN SPRING
Photographer—unknown

This group poses near the recently-discovered Lincoln
Spouting Spring on South Broadway. Barely visible is the
spouter, seen here in the middle of the photo behind the
fence. Discovered in 1896, the Lincoln would prove to be an
important find for its owners. Dozens of wells would be
drilled on the property in the years ahead in order to secure
the carbon dioxide gas trapped in the mineral water and hidden in vast caverns beneath the earth's surface. Signage on
the delivery wagon in the background indicates it belongs to
William Lindsay, a local grocer with a store at #4 Church
Street during the 90s. Like so many old photographs, no nota-
tions have been left to identify the individuals in the scene.
From their well- dressed appearance and new bikes, it would
seem that the bicyclists are from prosperous local families.

AFTER THE RAILROAD DEPOT FIRE
Photographer—unknown

Early in the morning of February 9, 1899, an important Victorian Saratoga landmark succumbed to flames. The handsome railroad station erected in 1871 was destroyed, along with the Sweeney Hotel across the Street and several other nearby buildings. The night watchman at the depot lost his life in the blaze. The depot had been the arrival point for most visitors in the post-war years, and the loss was mourned by Saratogians and returning tourists alike. Another station rose in its place, but the magnificent appearance and memories of the old depot would never be duplicated.

AFTER THE BROADWAY/CONGRESS STREET FIRE
Photographer—unknown

It seemed to many Saratogians that the southwest corner of Broadway and Congress Street was somehow cursed. The site had been the scene of too many horrible fires in the Victorian era, including devastating losses in 1864, '71 and '74. As the century concluded, the corner was again taken by flames on July 19, 1899. The fire began with a gasoline explosion in a bicycle shop, and the flames spread quickly, engulfing the Congress Park Hotel and the Favorite Spring Building. This photograph, believed to be the latest picture in this book, was taken on Broadway looking north, undoubtedly just shortly after the inferno was finally extinguished. In the background, the towers of the Grand Union Hotel are just visible.

CONGRESS HALL AND BROADWAY, LOOKING NORTH
Photographer—unknown

This photograph captures Broadway just before the turn of the century, at the end of the grand Victorian period. It is a setting which will be enjoyed by summer guests for only a few more years. The horse and buggy days are numbered, and Congress Hall unknowingly clings to a precarious existence.

CHAPTER 9

THE TWENTIETH CENTURY
The Landmarks Vanish

As the 21st century approaches, a visit to Saratoga Springs would prove frustrating for anyone in search of the wonderful buildings and places described in this book. Precious little of what is illustrated exists today. Adding to the frustration and the difficulty in trying to appreciate and understand the past is the fact that very few markers have been placed by succeeding generations to commemorate Saratoga's notable historic sites. On the surface, it would seem everything vanished without a trace.

The loss of Saratoga's glorious landmarks and heritage can be attributed to a variety of factors. As the village entered the 20th century, its economy still relied heavily on the summer tourist trade. Costly upkeep and rising taxes, coupled with increasingly inadequate revenues, spelled doom for many businesses. The Great Depression, a series of economic recessions, the closing of the gambling casinos, the temporary cessation of horse-racing and two world wars have all taken their toll on the economy and, therefore, the old environment.

The automobile has figured prominently in the demise of "old" Saratoga. The unpredictable and uncontrollable effects of nature have robbed Saratoga of further landmarks. Fires removed structures quickly, while wear and tear and decay worked its destruction more slowly.

As the new century began, the region's greatest natural resource, the mineral springs, were being destroyed by an industry which viewed the water merely as a supplier of gas. This, coupled with changing attitudes about the use of mineral water, relegated to the past that earlier scene of tiny picturesque spring pavilions and bottling houses.

The wholesale demise of Saratoga's 19th-century environment, however, did not go unnoticed. Many Saratogians and summer guests lamented the losses. An organized approach to stem the tide of destruction finally came, but unfortunately too late for many significant structures.

Although the magnificent Victorian hotels and lovely spring pavilions are long gone, a few reminders proudly hang on. The **Adelphi Hotel** and the **American Hotel** (now the **Rip**

Van Dam) stand prominently today on Broadway, still receiving summer guests as they always have. Scattered around the village are a few active public springs, reminders of an earlier day. The Hathorn, Congress and Old Red still rise from the depths, now under pleasant 20th-century covers, and still there are those who love the water and those who will have no taste of it whatsoever.

Throughout the city, a myriad of fine settings survived the intervening generations to provide that special charm which is such a landmark of Saratoga. Traveling through the older residential neighborhoods and streets today, one sees a pleasing medley of fine Victorian homes. Scattered among them are a few stately Greek Revival and Federal buildings, symbols of Saratoga's earlier times. From a more recent era, the late 1890s and the early 20th century, handsome Colonial Revival houses and small bungalows today appear old and historic and thus fit in nicely. Overall, a pleasant mix of architectural styles tells the story of Saratoga.

Broadway remains a thoroughfare envied by other communities, and the downtown environment is enjoyed by many thousands of visitors each year. The Collamer Block and Shackelford Block (Granite Palace) are handsome reminders of what the commercial environment was like a century ago. Other fine structures line the street as well.

But what about the sites pictured in this book? What happened to these examples of Victorian life and splendor?

THE HOTELS

Because of their size and impressive presence, probably the most obvious losses are the grand old hotels. Proclaimed during their heyday to be among the world's truly colossal palaces, they began to disappear shortly after the dawn of the 20th century. Nature took some of them in raging infernos, but many suffered a slower passing into history.

A new generation of vacationing tourists enjoyed the freedom and mobility offered by their automobiles. Across the nation, an exciting and expanding world of scenic places and enticing roadside attractions competed for attention and hard-earned dollars. Adventurous tourists, no longer confined to the places railroads took them, could now explore America on their own. Henry Ford put all of it within easy reach. For Saratoga's grand hotels, a decrease in patronage, and the tremendous costs involved in keeping up and operating the buildings, eventually led to their demise. The very nature of the Saratoga tourist season—essentially summers only—meant hotel owners had barely three months to generate income, while the ever-rising costs of upkeep, modernization and taxes were a year-round concern.

The first great wave of destruction came early in the century as one hotel after another was abandoned and slated for demolition. A marked drop in patronage was to blame. The Clarendon, Windsor, Congress, and Kensington were all leveled by 1915. It wasn't possible for all of the hotels to survive, and those that did had to find a niche. Small hotels and boarding houses on Saratoga's west side catered to African-Americans who came for relaxation and enjoyment or for summer employment. A few places were patronized primarily by Cubans and other Latins. Most numerous, however, were the new Jewish boarding houses and hotels. Immigrant European Jews in great numbers began to summer in Saratoga early in the 20th century. Drawn by the mineral springs and the promise of a summer of rest and relaxation similar to past experiences in the central European spas, Jews filled many of the old hotels and shops being vacated throughout the village. The buildings they bought and occupied were saved from certain demolition, at least for the time. During the 1950s and '60s trends would change again and many of these summer places closed for good.

Hotel construction continued in the new century, but buildings were smaller and less impressive than those of earlier generations. There was no longer a need for such large hotels. The craftsmanship and profuse ornamentation typical of high-Victorian architecture gave way to more modest facade adornment, partly as the result of a change in architectural trends, but also out of economic necessity. The old hotels had always endured competition, but in the 20th century roadside cabins and cottages, and then chain motels with modern conveniences like private baths and parking lots, were the latest trends.

What the wrecking ball wasn't taking, tragic fires were.

Some places were totally consumed, while others suffered less damage, only to be leveled afterwards. Throughout the century, the toll has been heavy, taking places like the Waverly, Columbian and Worden (Arlington House).

For these reasons, and many more, the great houses disappeared one by one. The following briefly describes what happened to some of those pictured in this book.

Congress Hall. The new century brought a precipitous drop in patronage, and with another temporary cessation of gambling early in the century, the hotel suddenly did not open for the summer season. Taken over by the city in 1911 for back taxes, Congress Hall was demolished in 1912/13, and the site was incorporated into a new city-owned Congress Park. A memorial to the late Spencer Trask was erected on the site, and its widely-acclaimed Spirit of Life, sculpted by Daniel Chester French, became a new village landmark. By the 1950s, a city library was serving the community on the corner of Broadway and Spring Street. The library recently moved to a new facility, and its former quarters on the Congress Hall site is now the home of the Saratoga County Arts Council.

Across Spring Street, the building which served as Congress Hall's ballroom still stands. Once the scene of wonderful parties and grand balls, the building was subsequently used as a dining and gambling establishment, a theater for stage productions, and a movie theater. Today, it is commercial space for a variety of businesses.

Anyone looking for the site of the old hotel will have to do some research to discover its location. There are no markers on the site to proclaim its glorious Victorian past, or its even more distant past when Gideon Putnam first began to erect a hotel here and died from the effort.

United States Hotel. This magnificent landmark hotel with its beautiful garden continued to be a popular destination for visitors drawn to the Saratoga season. There were still many glorious years at "the States" in the 20th century, but a slow irreversible decline was eventually brought on by its monstrous size and high operating expenses. The Victorian giant struggled to hang on, but the advent of WWII brought about a cessation of racing. The resulting lack of a strong summer season finally signaled the States' demise. Taken over by the city in 1943 for nonpayment of taxes, the hotel's elaborate furnishings were sold. Salvagers then took over and stripped the building of its copper, millions of bricks, acres of marble and countless fixtures. Picked clean, it was razed in 1946, leaving no sign that it had ever existed.

With the hotel, its beautiful interior garden park and century-old elm trees all gone, the property was eventually filled in by smaller commercial structures and a parking lot, in a manner which appears haphazard and out of character with much of the rest of downtown. Recently, the Wise Insurance office building was erected upon the site of the rear entrance to the States and is more in keeping with this historic site.

Fortunately, the old hotel setting can still be enjoyed, albeit vicariously. The States lives on in the big screen classic *Saratoga Trunk*, starring Gary Cooper and Ingrid Bergman.

Grand Union Hotel. Scene of many festive gatherings in the 20th century, the Grand Union survived longer than its main Victorian competitors. Though the aging structure had long required costly upkeep and its patronage was dwindling, it managed to cling precariously to life on its prime Broadway site. Several times in the 20th century, the grand old house was saved from impending demolition. Saratogians and summer guests alike voiced their support each time financial investors stepped in to save it. But the hotel could not escape the fact that it was a dinosaur in the age of the automobile.

The Grand Union's fate was finally sealed when federal and state investigations into organized crime resulted in the closure of Saratoga's gambling casinos in 1951. Deprived of the crowds drawn by gambling and night life, the hotel could no longer pay its way. The entire city was sent into an economic tailspin, and no one would step in to save the historic hotel.

At the conclusion of the racing season in 1952, the Grand Union's furnishings were offered at auction. A huge crowd witnessed the sad event. Saratogians, summer visitors, collectors and decorators from across the country bid on the hotel's many antique treasures. Thousands of Victorian sofas, tables, chairs and dressers were sold, along with enormous pier mirrors, chandeliers and decorative accessories. Marble top chests with mirrors reportedly passed the auction block for just ten dollars.

With its contents dispersed, wreckers methodically attacked the property. In the course of the following six months, the magnificent building was leveled, and a treasure was rendered into debris and rubble. Some of the combustibles were burned, but countless loads were suitable for "fill" and carted off somewhere to sculpt new terrain. The curious and heartbroken often stopped to watch the demolition, some taking photographs, others painting canvasses (as popular local artist Raymond Calkins did), to remember the mournful affair. Newspapers across the nation described the details and reminisced about times gone by. For the first time since Gideon Putnam built a tavern on the spot in 1802, the site was no longer capable of accommodating the summer traveler. One hundred and fifty years of glorious service had come to an end.

A strip shopping plaza and parking lot, looking every bit like any other plaza of the automobile age, eventually replaced the historic Grand Union Hotel. The land upon which Putnam, the Lelands and Stewart had built their dreams was now an unremarkable icon of a new age, anchored, ironically, by a Grand Union food store. Businesses, including the food chain, have come and gone from the prime commercial property over the past forty years, and periodically there has been talk of making something of the site again. A new commercial building is being erected on the southern portion of the property as this book is being written, but great expectations for the site remain unrealized.

Over a century ago, Americans across the nation were treated to daily newspaper accounts describing the festive summer activity here. Plantation owners in the south, merchants in Boston and financiers on Wall Street read the papers and planned their summer trips to the hotel. Mill workers in New England and farmers struggling on the Great Plains read or learned of these accounts as well. They too escaped their life of hard work, dreaming of the good times at the Grand Union. It was not just Saratoga's hotel, it was the nation's hotel. The location goes unrecognized, as no historical markers have been placed here.

Windsor Hotel. The beautiful Queen Anne-style hotel was demolished in 1914/15. Napoleon III had once been a summer guest in Saratoga. His magnificent portrait hung upon a wall at the Windsor. The painting was saved and today hangs prominently in the parlor of the Casino in Congress Park. With the hotel site cleared, it became a summer garden for a boarding house next door, the old Huestis House. Years later, the landscape changed again when a Holiday Inn and parking lot took over the site.

Clarendon Hotel. This was the only hotel on Broadway which long resisted the ostentatious architecture of the post-Civil War years, though it was eventually given a Victorian facade. The Clarendon, its park, and Washington Spring passed into memory after taking in its last guests during the 1902 summer season. The entire place was razed, and ownership passed to St. Peters Church located on the adjacent Broadway parcel. The ground lay vacant until it became the site of St. Peter's High School, and today continues as a site of education.

Columbian Hotel. The Columbian survived longer than many of the old houses on Broadway. In the 20th century, the New Columbian, as it was often called, catered to a Jewish clientele journeying for the rest and the water Saratoga offered. It was one of the largest houses operating with a Kosher kitchen. The hotel was destroyed by the so-called Convention Hall fire of 1965 and is now the site of a Friendly's ice cream shop and parking lot.

Waverly Hotel. Partially consumed by fire in 1914, its ruins were cleared away the following year. The site of this flat-iron-shaped building, and the nearby station of the Mt. McGregor Railroad, is near the busy intersection of the Route 50 Arterial and the beginning of North Broadway.

Arlington/Worden Hotel. The Arlington continued under the Worden banner and was an old favorite of locals and the summer crowd. Damage from a fire in 1961 led to the Worden's demise shortly thereafter. The Downtowner Hotel, a product of 1960s automobile architecture, sits upon this corner of Division Street and Broadway.

Mansion House/Excelsior Spring Hotel. The "country hotel" stood until 1967, when its furnishings were sold at auction and the building was razed. What had once been a picturesque country setting and park, a rural escape from the Victorian downtown, is today carved up and occupied by residential property, light industrial buildings, Community Health Plan offices, and the Route 50 highway as it heads northeast from the city.

Kensington Hotel. Just 27 years after the hotel opened in 1882 on Union Avenue, it was torn down. The site of this lovely, brick five-story hotel became part of the old Skidmore College campus, and today is the property of the Empire State College, which is about to build a new facility on the spot.

Crescent Hotel/Grand Central Hotel/Grand Central Block. The ill-fated southwest corner of Broadway and Congress Street was vacant at the turn of the century, as a fire in 1899 destroyed the businesses located there. A trolley station opened in April, 1916 on the site and was a busy center in the first half of the 20th century. By the 1940s the trolleys, too, were disappearing. The station today is popularly known as the Drink Hall, from its subsequent days of serving mineral water to the public. The building now houses the Urban Cultural Park and City Historian's office. Next door is a bank which shares the old hotel site.

Vermont House. In the 20th century, this guest house was operated as the Empire Hotel. Advertising brochures noted its beautiful patio, roof-garden solarium, and meals which were said to conform strictly to Jewish dietary law. Saratoga's decline in the 1950s and '60s and the Urban Renewal program of the '70s, swept it from its site on the corner of Grove Street and Maple Avenue. The site today is occupied by the Saratoga Springs City Center.

SPRINGS

As the 19th century was drawing to a close, the springs continued to have a large following. Baths were still very popular, and the water was widely consumed. The number of passionate devotees of the strict medical and water-cure regimes was, however, dwindling.

The search for new springs continued, but the businesses were not destined to become world-known baths and bottled waters, as similar enterprises of a time gone by. The sale of bottled mineral water was done more on a regional basis than on a national level. Intense competition from fresh and mineral springs elsewhere, and a myriad of soda fountain beverages now available, required Saratoga spring companies to re-evaluate their marketing strategies.

An ominous, but largely unrecognized, threat was affecting the mineral springs at the turn of the century. The peril would forever alter the community. It started harmlessly enough in the 1890s when the country's thirst was increasingly being quenched by flavored carbonated water, commonly known as soda pop. Saratoga's waters contained an abundant supply of an ingredient vital to the soda industry. Bottlers needed carbon dioxide gas to give their product that unique effervescence and bubbling action that is still enjoyed by soda drinkers today, and mineral water brought to the surface readily yielded this trapped gas.

With the ingredient freely available in Saratoga, carbonic acid gas companies moved in to siphon off the resource. The firms drilled wells and erected plants with huge holding tanks to collect the gas. South of the village, in the geysers area, the once picturesque landscape took on the appearance of an unsightly manufacturing complex as tanks, pipes and factory buildings appeared. This new drain on Saratoga's resources was far beyond what had ever been taken from the earth before. Millions of gallons of water were wasted.

During their explorations, the gas companies unexpectedly discovered "dry gas" wells beneath Saratoga. Previously-unknown, huge underground caverns of gas lay hidden beneath the region, exploding with tremendous force when revealed by a drill bit. Deep well pumps and miles of pipe controlled the extraction, but nature's underground balance was thrown into disarray. Suddenly, what had appeared a seemingly endless resource prior to the 1890s was proving all too finite, as many mineral water wells around the city began to dry up.

Concerned Saratogians turned to the New York State Legislature, and in 1909 it proposed the creation of a State Reservation at Saratoga Springs designed to help protect the springs from further exploitation. With funds provided by the state, the principal springs around the village were purchased from private owners over the next few years. South of the village, where the gas plants had so depleted the resources, a huge tract of land came under state ownership. With the gas companies closed, and numerous wells capped, everyone hoped the subterranean water system would be restored. Scientists surmised that given time, the mineral springs would eventually replenish themselves and again flow to the surface under the pressure of built-up gas.

In the following years, under guidance from the State Reservation, the springs were carefully developed and used. In the city, a publicly-owned Congress Park began to take shape, as did a park around the historic High Rock cone. South of the village, efforts began to unfold which would eventually lead to a large and wonderful new spa and park for the city.

VILLAGE SPRINGS AND PARKS

Significant changes came to the old spa and mineral spring operations when the State took over most of the springs in the village. Most familiar was the development of Congress Park and High Rock Park.

High Rock Spring. This historic spring continued in operation until 1904. A few years later, the land around the cone was taken over by the city when the State Reservation gained control. The bottling house and eagle-topped pavilion were razed, and a small cover was built over the High Rock, which became the focal point of the small park at the historic site. High Rock itself ceased flowing long ago, but in the 1970s, renewed interest led to a new search for mineral water. The historic cone was made to flow again with water piped from another spring. As a sad testament to the times, this historic site, like others in the city, suffers from occasional vandalism and the indifference of a new era. The ancient village brook which once flowed past this site is now contained deep below the ground, confined by a concrete drainage system. Across the street, the old Magnetic Spring and High Rock Bathhouse, as well as the railroad tracks once found here, are gone, and the area is home to Spring Valley Apartments.

Seltzer Spring. Maps from the turn of the century note that the Seltzer's brick bottling house, located next to the High Rock, was being used as a storage warehouse. However, the place was eventually razed when the property became part of the new High Rock Park. A modern mineral water fountain sits in front of the site offering Peerless and Governor springwater. A picturesque pavilion reminiscent of Saratoga's earlier days is presently being erected over the two springs.

Star Spring. The Star pavilion and bottling house near the High Rock were also razed to become part of the small park. Few who walk the grounds of the park today could ever imagine the activity that once took place here. A century ago, Star Spring water was available in bottles and as draft dispensed from oak barrels at soda fountains and drugstores around the country. Star Spring mineral water bottles, like the bottles from each of the other springs of the Victorian period, are actively sought by collectors. The "Saratogas," as the bottles are generally referred to, are among the few tangible reminders that some of these springs ever existed.

United States and Pavilion Springs. Long ago capped, abandoned and razed, the springs and their decorative

Victorian pavilion are today the site of commercial enterprise. Bill's Mobil, a gas station and truck rental company, is closest to the United States/Pavilion site, and next door, a restaurant, the Parting Glass, stands on the location of the Royal Spring, which also operated here in the late 19th and early 20th century.

Empire Spring. The popular spring continued in business until just after the turn of the century, when the Clark Textile Company purchased the bottling plant and converted it into a textile mill. The factory expanded over the years and was taken over by the Van Raalte Company, which continued to operate it as a textile mill. The old Empire Spring flowed inside, and for years factory employees were said to continue drinking the water. The factory closed in 1986, and the building was abandoned. Today, the derelict factory sits in wait for some new use. The cast iron lions which guarded this spring in the 19th century were "discovered" inside the building a couple of years ago and entrusted to a local preservation group.

Old Red Spring. Patrons still stop at the Old Red, though they arrive in cars rather than by horse and carriage. One of the few active old mineral springs in the city, the Old Red Spring has now been used for over two hundred years. Its bath facility was razed in 1912. People may still be seen carrying jugs of the precious resource to their vehicles, and some occasionally rub the water over their face and body, just as did John Morrissey and countless others who bathed here long ago.

Excelsior Spring. At the turn of the century, the Lawrence family continued to own the spring and the nearby Mansion House/Excelsior Spring Hotel. In 1888, the family had diversified and opened a bank supply and printing company here. Known as C. W. Lawrence Bank Supplies, they shipped moneybags, coin wrappers and office supplies from the site to banks around the country. Their bottling plant became known in the 20th century as the Saratoga Quevic Company, offering a variety of beverages. The various businesses and properties changed hands over the years. The Quevic operation ended in a huge explosion and fire in February, 1966. Fortunately, the classic Excelsior Spring pavilion escaped disaster, and was saved for future generations when it was moved to the Saratoga Race Course. There,

the original Excelsior pavilion sits atop the Big Red Spring. In recent years, a new Excelsior Spring Water Company was formed and began distributing fresh, non-mineral water from the old site. Other than its name and location, it has no affiliation with its historic mineral spring namesake.

Eureka Spring and White Sulphur Spring. A lovely park surrounding these springs was well attended in the first half of the 20th century. Autos drove out Lake Avenue and turned down Eureka Park Road to visit the popular destination, called the Saratoga Sulphur and Mud Baths. All manner of therapeutic baths and treatments were offered during the summers, but its mud baths, taken in the old bath house, were a particularly popular feature. The end came when a fire struck on October 29, 1958. Today, all that remains of the park, bathhouse, springs, and railroad whistle stop once found here, are the dilapidated remnants of the original Eureka Spring pavilion, a decaying pile of rubble at the end of Eureka Avenue. Thick undergrowth, brush, trees, and a swamp render the area almost impenetrable, and it is difficult to imagine this had once been a carefully tended garden park.

Hathorn Spring. Henry Hathorn's name lives on in Saratoga because a bit of luck during a construction project revealed this precious spring. When the State Reservation took over the springs, it kept open Hathorn's vintage drink hall. The facility was very popular, and countless thousands continued to visit the site. But, in 1937 the lovely old building was partially destroyed by fire, then, in 1941, totally razed. Most of the land today is used as a parking lot. The water is still available beneath a pavilion reminiscent of the Victorian days. The Hathorn remains very popular and enjoys an active local following. Its location alongside Congress Park and the downtown parking lots makes it especially accessible for tourists and residents.

White Sulphur Spring (Saratoga Lake). South of Snake Hill, as Route 9P winds its way around Saratoga Lake, the remains of a rustic pavilion sit alongside the road. The tiny neglected structure once housed the lake country's White Sulphur Spring. The hotel and bathhouses are long gone, and the site is now traveled over daily by countless cars on the lake road.

CONGRESS SPRING AND PARK

Throughout the 19th and early 20th century, all of the present-day park was privately owned. The modern public park consists of three distinct parcels: the original Congress Park (covering all the land lying south of Congress Street); the Congress Hall and bottling works site (the northwestern portion up to Spring Street); and the Morrissey/Canfield Club House and grounds (the northeastern section extending up to Spring Street and over to Circular Street).

Original Congress Park site. A new era began in 1909 when legislation was enacted which led to the establishment of the State Reservation. In 1910, permission was gained to give the village bonding authority to purchase the park. Then, in early 1911, the park grounds were officially transferred to the village. Saratogians could finally rightfully say it was their park. Plans were drawn up for the site, including landscaping and a new lake. During the next decade, the beautiful Victorian arcade began to disappear from the scene. It was as fragile as it was decorative. Constant use and the weather of the north country were wearing on the structure. Architectural styles were changing, and the old Gothic was no longer appreciated. Plans called for change, and because the public park would grow to be much larger than it was originally, the city park no longer needed this entry to the grounds. First to disappear was the entrance to the Victorian arcade, soon followed by the delightful portion over the Congress.

Once the arcade was razed, Congress Spring was given an open fountain. Set in a small depression in which patrons stepped down to take the water, it appeared somewhat like a sunken garden. A small canopy sheltered the spring fountain. Though still pleasant, it was not like the magnificent Victorian, nor the lovely classic structure the public had associated with the Congress. The Gothic arcades covering the Columbian Spring and, at the opposite end, the cafe section remained for a time, but they too were eventually razed.

In the 20th century, the flow of the Congress was often inconsistent and not as voluminous as in the past. Problems associated with the gas company days, and occasional contamination, required re-tubing. In 1939, Congress Spring was abandoned by the state, and the sunken garden was unceremoniously filled in with rock and rubble, reportedly prompted by a dispute between the city and the state. It appeared,

at least to those who noticed and cared, that the long and important history of Congress Spring had come to an end.

During this period, other features of the Victorian park fell into disrepair and disappeared. Benches, chairs, cast-iron urns and statues slipped from the scene. Occasionally, new features took their place. In 1922, a monumental granite gateway honoring Katrina Trask was added as a back entrance to the park. Another new stone gateway at the park's main entrance memorialized Senator Brackett, who passionately worked to rescue the mineral springs by securing legislation creating the State Reservation. The fanciful Victorian bandstand at lake side was removed, and a new memorial was erected in 1931 honoring local war veterans.

Morrissey/Canfield Club House and Grounds. Richard Canfield was ambitiously redecorating the Club House and adding new property to his grounds early in the 20th century. He bought the old Indian Encampment property, and another piece which had long been occupied by a huge building referred to as "the Casino," which had burned in 1901. Upon this ground, Canfield created a lovely Italian garden. Adorned with finely-carved marble statuary, a wonderful fountain, shrubs and flowers, the spot became a new Saratoga treasure.

The Club House was enlarged with a new dining room and kitchen. Canfield spared no expense, incorporating leaded stained glass panels, parquet floors and mahogany woodwork. The house prospered under Canfield's ownership, but with another cessation of gambling in 1907, it lay dormant. Canfield attempted to sell the place, but found no buyer until 1910, when the village bought his property for $150,000. Canfield sold the furnishings at auction in May that year, and the grounds and Club House later became part of Congress Park. Only afterwards did the gaming Club House become known as "Canfield Casino."

Congress Hall Site. The misfortunes at Congress Hall provided more property for Saratoga's new park. Burdened by expensive upkeep and taxes, and fewer patrons, the beautiful Victorian hotel was doomed. It was taken over by the city for back taxes in 1911, and two years later, the hotel was razed. The hotel site, razed sections along old Putnam Street behind the hotel, including the **Hamilton Spring** and the site of the Congress Spring bottling plant, were incorporated into Congress Park. Putnam Street was eliminated between

Congress and Spring Street. Shortly thereafter, the Spencer Trask Memorial Fountain was added to the grounds of Congress Park. The Civil War memorial statue was moved from Broadway onto the site in 1921, when aging veterans and others thought it best removed from encroaching automobiles.

Modern Park. With the addition of Canfield's property, and then the Congress Hall site, the park had grown to its present dimensions, covering an area roughly twice as large as the old private park of the 19th century. The park was in jeopardy of losing ground in the late 1950s: after the demise of the Grand Union Hotel, some local businessmen and civic leaders looked to the park as a potential site for a new hotel, and plans were drawn up for a large hotel and parking lot on land behind the Casino. Historically-minded citizens thought it an outrage, and the plan was hotly debated on the streets and in the press. Approval was given by the voters but, fortunately, the plan was never carried out. Congress Park was spared.

Congress Park in the 1990s contains a mix of features from its long and colorful past. Some vestiges and reminders stand prominently, while others offer only a glimpse of the past. Standing distinctively at its center is the Casino. The brick building became home to the Historical Society of Saratoga Springs which operates a museum dedicated to the preservation and interpretation of the history of the city. Inside are many treasures from Saratoga's past. The facility is also used for social functions and is frequently the site of lavish gatherings, just as in days gone by. In the 1970s, a renewed interest in the historical site led to another search for a mineral spring. With a vein secured, a reproduction spring pavilion was erected on the site of the Congress in 1976, the nation's bicentennial and the hundredth anniversary of the demise of the original pavilion. The handsome new setting harks back to days long ago when Dr. John Clarke was owner of the spring. The Columbian Spring also has a pleasant new pavilion, but attempts to adequately secure the flow of the mineral spring have proven futile.

The huge old pines and oaks growing on the high ground of the park must be similar to what Clarke and others found here in the early days. Elsewhere, the cast-iron urns and fountains remind us of Saratoga's vibrant heyday in the Victorian era when the park was transformed into a picturesque fanciful wonderland. Though no longer the artful setting it was when Canfield created it, the Italian garden and its often-admired fountain, "Spit and Spat," is still a popular attraction, as are the brilliantly-colored flowers planted here each year.

Still one of the most popular spots in the city, Congress Park remains important to the social fabric of the community.

GEYSERS REGION—A NEW SPA AND PARK

The development of a new Saratoga environment commenced when the State began to acquire the assets of the gas companies south of the village. With the land and mineral springs eventually in state hands, two separate parks, Lincoln Park and Geyser Park, were laid out. Efforts at developing a new world-class spa began when Dr. Simon Baruch arrived on the scene and became actively engaged in studying the medicinal waters. By 1912, Baruch had begun his investigations in earnest and worked tirelessly in reestablishing Saratoga as a world-class health spa. Baruch had long advocated the benefits of mineral water therapy, had been a professor of hydrotherapy at Columbia University's College of Physicians and Surgeons, and was familiar with the great spas of Europe. For the next decade, he tirelessly pursued his dream, encouraged largely by the Jewish clientele still actively supporting the mineral springs.

Baruch passed away before his plans were realized, but his dream for Saratoga was carried out by one of his sons, Bernard Baruch. With an interest and enthusiasm for the water inspired by his father, the younger Baruch pursued the concept of a new spa at Saratoga under authority from Franklin Delano Roosevelt, then governor of New York. Baruch headed a commission which studied the concept, ultimately resulting in the establishment of the Spa, which opened to the public in the summer of 1935. The new Spa's park-like grounds, its Roosevelt, Washington and Lincoln bathhouses, Hall of Springs, and Simon Baruch Laboratory established Saratoga once again as the principal spa in the United States. A brand new hotel, appropriately named the Gideon Putnam, provided the perfect place to stay while enjoying the waters. The setting provided ample opportunity for pleasant walks and outdoor activities—indispensable ingredients of a therapeutic approach to good health. The initial two parks located here had evolved into a single contiguous unit and grown much larger than imagined in earlier days.

With the opening of the State Reservation Spa, the beginning of a new era was anxiously anticipated by enthusiasts of the springs. New springs had been tapped, and modern bathhouses offered relaxation and treatment. The water was again being bottled under the new authority, and springs like Geyser, Coesa, and State Seal were marketed. The facilities were well patronized, but the expected glorious new era never materialized. As the years went by, there was a decline in patronage.

Bureaucrats and politicians in Albany, in tight fiscal times, looked on a "luxury" like the spa as an easy target for budget cuts. Some components of the park, like the new hotel and the summer theater, did do well, but the spa came to be used more as a day recreational facility, popular for its picnic facilities, swimming pools and golf courses.

A new era for the park began in the summer of 1966 when the Saratoga Performing Arts Center opened. Today, entertainment at SPAC draws hundreds of thousands to the grounds. At the baths, however, patronage continued to fall. Despite this, the Lincoln was restored and today is used for park administrative offices and for mineral baths. The Washington has been turned into the home of the National Museum of Dance. The Roosevelt Bath is presently being restored to provide visitors an opportunity to experience the pleasures of a mineral bath.

The Spa has evolved into the present State Park, with an emphasis on recreation and entertainment. The aging brick State Reservation buildings of the 1930s already look like antiquated and majestic examples of another by-gone era. Much of the park is forested, leaving virtually no indication that this was a monstrous industrial site early in the 1900s, or that, over a century ago, the land was clear and homes, farms, fields, springs, bottling houses, small hotels and businesses were located here. One would be hard pressed to imagine trains and trolleys stopping here to discharge passengers eagerly seeking an afternoon of fun, rest and relaxation. Sadly, no historical markers commemorate those wonderful 19th-century landmarks.

WHAT HAPPENED TO SOME OF THE INDIVIDUAL SPRINGS PICTURED IN THIS BOOK?

Geyser Spring. The Geyser still bubbled up from the depths, and its large brick bottling house remained open after the State took it over. It continued to be a very popular day use facility. But with a new State Spa bottling plant erected nearby, the Victorian building was used for storage and other purposes. In the 1960s, the old Geyser was razed when a new highway from Saratoga to Ballston rendered the site unrecognizable. Filled in and paved over, the setting became a section of Route 50, just a few yards from the traffic light at Geyser Road. Underground piping took the popular Geyser water to the State Reservation bottling house not far from the original site. Today, it flows from a spigot outside the facility. Nearby, pleasant little Geyser Lake is much smaller than it was a century ago, with portions which are now more swamp, mud and cattails than lake.

Triton Spring. This spring was located across Geyser Lake from the Vichy, and nearby was a small boarding house called the Triton House. The location is long gone, hidden somewhere along the highway and State Park property just north of the Geyser Road traffic light at Route 50.

Champion Spouting Spring. In the 1870s and 1880s, huge crowds enjoyed the Champion when it was heralded as the most powerful spouting spring in the eastern United States. As the 20th century began, a gas collection facility loomed near the old bottling house and an ancient grist mill powered in earlier times by Geyser Creek. The magnificent spouter was capped early in the century, and control of the site passed to the State Reservation. Everything was eventually razed as the site became part of the new spa park. For a time the "New Champion" spouted nearby, but it was only a feeble reminder of the original. The Champion's location lies behind, and just west of, the Saratoga Performing Arts Center stage. When crossing the bridge high over Geyser Creek to enter SPAC today, visitors see the site as they gaze upstream to the north, but there is no indication whatsoever that the Champion Spouting Spring ever existed.

Vichy Spring. The Vichy was the one commercial spring which remained in private hands and did not become a part of the State Park. The highly-regarded Vichy is probably the most widely-recognized Saratoga mineral water of the 20th century. In the 19th, the Vichy was popular, but did not enjoy as large a following as the Geyser, Hathorn, Congress and others. But from the 1890s on, its popularity increased dramatically, and in the 20th century, bottles have been sold across the country. The bottling plant was enlarged and altered, and the process modernized, as ownership changed over the years. The front portion of the original, extended pavilion porch can still be seen at the plant now bottling "Saratoga Water."

OTHER PLACES AND BUILDINGS

Saratoga Race Course. The summer racing meets are undoubtedly one of the most widely-recognized features of 20th-century Saratoga. Long known as the oldest race track in America, exhaustive research by Ed Hotaling identified the existing facility as the oldest still in use in the country for any sport, not just the sport of horse-racing. The earliest grandstand at the Course stood for nearly three decades, until it was enlarged and re-designed in 1892 by Gottfried Walbaum. It is his remake of the grandstand (with many later alterations) which still greets visitors today, a century later.

Walbaum's years at the helm were turbulent and troubling, and the seasonal racing meets experienced a precipitous decline in prestige and importance. But in 1901, William C. Whitney arrived on the scene, and horse owners, racing enthusiasts and Saratogians would forever be grateful. Whitney headed a new association of owners who worked diligently to restore the Saratoga racing season back to the preeminent place it held in earlier times. They improved the track facilities and the racing surface. Walbaum's grandstand was enlarged in 1902. It was cut into three sections, then moved and "stretched" to accommodate larger crowds while retaining its Queen Anne character. Whitney helped reinstate integrity and respectability in Saratoga racing, and was thereby able to accomplish the vital restoration of stakes races, heftier purses and a return of the best horses and their owners.

The meets have had ups and downs over the years since and have, on a couple occasions, been halted by war or investigations into gambling. But great horses have raced on this ground, and the track's reputation as the "graveyard of favorites" has been borne out time and time again by the emptied wallets of many and the enriched pockets of a few.

The concerns people had over horse-wagering have largely passed. Parlor and casino gambling, on the other hand, was done away with in 1951, but the prospect of its return fuels an unending debate. Today, when people complain about the track, it is likely the inevitable traffic which clogs the city streets each August which raises their ire. Hundreds of thousands of people from all walks of life pass through the turnstiles each season. The historic racing meet endures as a vital economic resource and immense source of pride for the community.

Town Hall. City Hall, as it is now called, still serves the residents of Saratoga as their house of government. In 1936, in fear that the weight of the large brass bell housed in the clock tower could cause the tower's collapse, the entire top portion was dismantled. Its loss rendered a magnificent and proud building far less grand and distinguishable. The cast-iron lions placed in front of the building when it was erected in 1871 were removed at the same time. Today, the lions can be found alongside wading pools in city recreation parks on the east and west sides. In recent years, the theater inside the Hall was restored and is again used for performances, as it was long ago.

Saratoga Lake Region. Virtually all of the 19th-century lake country landmarks have disappeared over the years. The land around the lake was mostly carved up for housing, much of it for vacation cottages, but the area continues to be an important recreation setting and home to numerous restaurants.

Throughout the first half of the 20th century, the lake region was well known for its night clubs and gambling casinos, until a federal investigation shut them down in 1951. Newman's, Riley's, Arrowhead, Meadowbrook and Piping Rock were some of the popular clubs of that era, often playing host to well-known entertainers of stage and screen. Kaydeross Park was a favorite lake-side attraction for families which swam along its beach and enjoyed its amusement rides and games. The amusement park and the casinos are all gone now. The original **Moon's Lake House** was destroyed by fire in May, 1893 and replaced by another building which burned in 1926. Other restaurants were built upon the property, some of which took the old Moon's Lake House name. The rustic-style buildings and park-like grounds **Frank Leslie** once owned along the lake have vanished, but the name he gave his property, Interlaken, lives on in a pleasant group of residences built between Saratoga Lake and Lake Lonely. **White Sulphur Spring Hotel** had a rich and colorful history in the 20th century until it, too, was leveled. Nothing about the present site would lead one to suspect that boxers Jack Dempsey and Gene Tunney trained there, or that wealthy, influential and famous people once passed their afternoons and evenings sipping champagne here. The site today is pierced by Route 9P wrapping its way around the lake. Scattered among all the vacation housing along the lake, a few period Victorian cottages can be spotted, though more often than not, they have been remodeled and have lost their Victorian form.

Railroad Station. The handsome Victorian railroad depot was destroyed by fire in 1899. As a rail station was vital to the village economy, shortly thereafter a new Delaware and Hudson Railroad station sprang up on the same spot. That facility was active in the heart of the city until the late 1950s when the lines were abandoned and a small stop was built on tracks skirting Saratoga's west side. Today, the line carries more freight than passengers. With the removal of the old downtown tracks and station, the space was freed up for streets (Railroad Place), parking lots, and a large grocery store now operated by the Price Chopper chain.

Glen Mitchell Hotel. The old hotel closed in 1886 and became the Redemptorist Mission House and a school. These operated for many years at the site, but were abandoned when St. Clement's Church built a new facility on Lake Avenue. The remains of the old Glen Mitchell House disappeared over the years, along with the old toboggan slide and vestiges of the outbuildings used in the days when the county agricultural fairs were held here. The city school district's Maple Avenue Middle School was erected on the property a few years ago.

Chancellor Walworth's Home. The Chancellor's family had long since replaced his early home with a sprawling Queen Anne residence by the time the 20th century arrived. Early in the new century, it was used as a hotel, but historical records and furnishings from the Chancellor's days remained inside. In 1952, Clara Walworth, the last of the Chancellor's heirs, passed away, transferring by her will many of the treasures to a trust. That trust maintains and displays the holdings at the Walworth Memorial Museum housed on the third floor of the Casino. In 1955, the derelict mansion was torn down. The Broadway site is presently occupied by a gas station situated between buildings known as the Old Community Theater and Old Firehouse.

Temple Grove This building still graces the corner of Circular and Spring Street, though it now no longer wears its observation deck and cupola which were added in the days when Dr. Charles Dowd ran the seminary. Early in the 20th century, it was purchased by Lucy Scribner, who operated the Young Women's Industrial Club. Scribner later turned it over to what became known as Skidmore College. Home to apartment dwellers today, it takes its name, Skidmore Apartments, from its many years of service boarding Skidmore College students.

Today, the site goes unrecognized for its important earlier days when young Victorian women were educated here, and few remember that the founder of modern time zones, a system used around the world, once owned the place and worked on his radical ideas to standardize time keeping. It is even harder yet to envision how the setting looked in 1840 when tall native trees still grew here and the site was considered the outskirts of a very small village. That year, orator Daniel Webster stood upon this ground and spoke to a crowd of 10,000 assembled for a Whig Party gathering to hear talk of presidential politics and "Tippecanoe and Tyler Too."

OTHERS

The large, brick **First Methodist Church** on Washington Street still receives the faithful, though today's congregants are Baptists.

The handsome **Lester residence** on North Broadway was replaced earlier in the century by a post-Victorian home.

The **residence on Circular Street**, sitting across from Congress Park, looks very much like it did a century ago.

Dr. Strong's Remedial Institute vanished from Circular Street. A modern building was erected on the site of the old sanitarium when Skidmore College operated its downtown campus. That building is now used for apartments.

The commercial block on Broadway just south of City Hall still stands proud and prominent. A product of Seymour Ainsworth in 1871, the Italian-style building has been largely restored and is a wonderful reminder of the type of commercial buildings once found all along the main street. The drug store at its north end, Menges and Curtis, is one of only a very few local establishments which can trace its name, location and business activity all the way back to the same location in the Victorian heyday.

OTHERS MENTIONED,
BUT NOT PICTURED IN THE BOOK

The main residence and many outbuildings and cottages of Judge Henry Hilton's estate, **Woodlawn**, are long gone. After the Judge passed away, the place was abandoned, neglected, vandalized, burned and razed. The rambling estate is now occupied by new buildings in the form of a modern campus for Skidmore College.

Convention Hall on Broadway was scene to many noteworthy events in the late 19th century and throughout much of the 20th century. The people of Saratoga were robbed of their much-loved center and concert hall when a devastating fire in 1965 consumed it and the Columbian Hotel across the street. Today, the site is occupied by the YMCA.

Franklin Smith's interesting creation on Broadway, the **House of Pansa**, went bankrupt early in the new century. It became home to a Masonic Temple and Jewish synagogue. Most recently, it has become a nicely-restored setting for offices and commercial businesses. Interestingly, the dreamer Smith went to Washington, D.C., and stirred things up there as well. He proposed a colossal rebuilding of the District, and legislation was even introduced into Congress to study and implement some of his plans. Less visionary minds prevailed, Smith was again labeled a lunatic by some, and again his visions were abandoned.

CONCLUSION

This has been a sample of the Saratoga scene in the post-Civil War days. Only a few of the places illustrated have survived the passage of time. Many others not pictured here were constructed during the 19th century and live on, lining the streets of the city today. Each has its own link to the past.

Many caring residents today work earnestly restoring and preserving Saratoga's past. Some return grandeur to old homes, while others advocate for the springs, volunteer on historical projects or help at a museum or library. While it is lamentable that much of what is pictured here is gone, Saratogians can and should be proud of their historic community. Saratoga wears this history well. There is much to be admired in this small city, and a stroll along Broadway or a walk through the old residential neighborhoods bears that out. Each place has its own story to tell, for this is a city of many stories—some well-known, and others still waiting to be told.

The summer season bustles today just as it always has, and visitors swell the streets and sidewalks. But guests no longer come just in the summers. Saratogians have worked hard to make the city a year-round destination. Visitors come to enjoy concerts, picnics, conventions, lectures and street fairs. They enjoy Saratoga's shops, restaurants, night life, horse races, and a host of other activities making up the year-round "Saratoga scene." There are even those who still journey for the mineral water which continues to bubble up from beneath the earth, for Saratoga is, after all, Saratoga *Springs*.

CHAPTER NOTES

1. Haydon,Roger, *Upstate Travels: British Views of Nineteenth-Century New York,* 109,110.

2. Colt, Mrs. S.S., *The Tourist's Guide Through the Empire State,* 137.

3. *Saratoga Illustrated: The Visitor's Guide to Saratoga Springs,* 1882 edition, 5, 8-11.

4. *Ibid.,* 33-34, 36-37, 43-44,59.

5. Child,Hamilton, *Gazetteer and Business Directory of Saratoga County, Queensbury, Warren County for 1871,* 204.

6. "Red Spring Register", August 20, 1876, unnumbered.

7. *Saratoga Illustrated: The Visitor's Guide to Saratoga Springs,* 1882 edition, 45-46, 81-82.

8. *Ibid.,* 15.

9. *The Daily Saratogian,* September 19, 1870, 3.

10. Durkee, Cornelius, *Reminiscences of Saratoga,* 135,136.

11. Sylvester, Nathaniel, *History of Saratoga County, New York,* 1878, 168.

12. *The Daily Saratogian,* July 28, 1879, 2.

13. *Saratoga Illustrated: The Visitor's Guide to Saratoga Springs,* 1882 edition, 97, 98, 99.

14. *Ibid.,* 83.

15. *Ibid.,* 131.

16. *The Daily Saratogian,* April 29, 1872, 3.

17. *Saratoga Illustrated: The Visitor's Guide to Saratoga Springs,* 1882 edition, 107.

18. Colt, Mrs. S.S., *The Tourist's Guide Through the Empire State,* 147,148.

19. *The Saratogian Almanac,* "1896 Illustrated Yearbook", unnumbered page 6.

20. Waller, George, *Saratoga: Saga of an Impious Era,* 233.

21. *Ibid.,* 233.

22. *Souvenir of Floral Festival No.1 and Prospectus of a Greater Saratoga with Views and Plans of Proposed Park,* 24.

SOURCES CONSULTED

Published Sources:

Allen, Richard L. *A Historical, Chemical and Theraputic Analysis of the the Principal Mineral Fountains at Saratoga Springs.* Saratoga Springs, N.Y.: B. Huling, 1844.

Allen, Richard L. *Handbook of Saratoga and Stranger's Guide.* New York, N.Y.: W.H. Arthur & Co., 1859.

Britten, Evelyn Barrett. *Chronicles of Saratoga.* Saratoga Springs, N.Y.: Evelyn Barrett Britten, 1959.

Boyd's Saratoga Springs Directory. Saratoga Springs, N.Y.: Fred Boyd, 1868, 1872, 1874, 1876, 1878, 1879, 1880.

Butler, Benjamin C. *The Summer Tourist: Descriptive of the Delaware and Hudson Canal Co.'s Railroads and Their Summer Resorts.* Boston, Ma.: Franklin Press, 1880.

Carola, Chris and Mastrianni, Beverly and Noonan, Michael. *George Bolster's Saratoga Springs.* Saratoga Springs, N.Y.: The Donning Company, 1990.

Charter of the Village of Saratoga Springs. Saratoga Springs, N.Y.: Board of Trustees, Village of Saratoga Springs, 1887.

Child, Hamilton, ed. *Gazetteer and Business Directory of Saratoga County, and Queensbury, Warren County for 1871.* Syracuse, N.Y.: Hamilton Child, 1871.

Colt, Mrs. S.S. *The Tourist's Guide Through the Empire State.* Albany, N.Y.: Mrs. S.S. Colt, 1871.

Dahl, Curtis. "Mr. Smith's American Acropolis", *American Heritage,* June 1956.

The Daily Saratogian. Saratoga Springs, N.Y.: The Saratogian, 1870-1881 and 1887-1890.

Darrah, William Culp. *Stereo Views: A History of Stereographs in America and Their Collection.* Gettysburg, Pa.: Times and News Publishing Co., 1964.

Darrah, William Culp. *The World of Stereographs.* Gettysburg, Pa.: W.C. Darrah, 1977.

Davison, Gideon M. *The Fashionable Tour: A Guide to the Travellers Visiting the Middle and Northern States and the Provinces of Canada,* 4th Edition. Saratoga Springs, N.Y.: Gideon M. Davison, 1830.

Davison, Gideon M. *The Traveller's Guide Through the Middle and Northern States and the Provinces of Canada.* 6th Edition. Saratoga Springs, N.Y.: G.M. Davison, 1834.

Dearborn, R.F. *Saratoga and How to See It.* Saratoga Springs, N.Y.: R.F. Dearborn, 1871.

Dearborn, R.F. *Saratoga and How to See It.* Saratoga Springs, N.Y.: C.D. Slocum, 1872.

Dearborn, R.F. *Saratoga and What to See There: An Annual Guide with a Treatise on the Mineral Waters.* New York, N.Y.: R.F. Dearborn, 1874.

"Diary, Daniel Benedict, April 9, 1819-November 30, 1865", *Saratoga Sentinel.* Saratoga Springs, N. Y.: Saratoga Sentinel, 1881.

Durkee, Cornelius. *Reminiscences of Saratoga.* Saratoga Springs, N.Y.: The Saratogian, 1928.

Farmers' Pocket Directory and Map of Saratoga County, N.Y., 1890. Valatie, N. Y.: Lant and Silvernail, 1890.

Fuller, Edward. *Our Thoroughfare, Past and Present Reminiscences, 1819-1918.* Saratoga Springs, N.Y.: Saratoga Sun, series publication 1918-19.

Gilbert, George. *Photography: The Early Years, A Historical Guide for Collectors.* New York, N.Y.: Harper and Row, Publishers, 1980.

The Grant Cottage Chronicles. Saratoga Springs, N.Y.: The Friends of Ulysses S. Grant Cottage, Vol. 7 #1, Spring 1996.

Greater Saratoga Directory for 1895. Saratoga Springs, N.Y.: Mingay and Reagan, 1895.

Haydon, Roger. *Upstate Travels: British Views of Nineteenth-Century New York.* Syracuse, N.Y.: Syracuse University Press, 1982.

Hotaling, Edward. *They're Off! Horse Racing at Saratoga.* Syracuse, N.Y.: Syracuse University Press, 1995.

Huling's Saratoga Springs Directory. Saratoga Springs, N.Y.: Huling and Company, 1881, 1882.

Illustrated Combination Atlas of Saratoga and Ballston. New York, N.Y.: J. B. Beers & Co., 1876.

Jensen, Oliver and Kerr, Joan Paterson and Belsky, Murray. *American Album.* American Heritage Publishing Co., 1968.

Kemp, James F. *The Mineral Springs of Saratoga.* Albany, N.Y.: New York State Museum, 1912.

Kettlewell, James K. *Saratoga Springs: An Architectural History.* Saratoga Springs, N.Y.: Lyrical Ballad Bookstore, 1991.

Lee, Henry, ed. *Lee's Guide to Saratoga, the Queen of Spas.* New York, N.Y.: Henry Lee, 1885.

McLaren, Daniel. *The Pavilion Fountain at Saratoga.* New York, N.Y.: Daniel McLaren, 1841.

Merrill, Arthur A. *Confessions of Congress Park.* Chappaqua, N.Y.: Analysis Press, 1955.

New Topographical Atlas of Saratoga Co. New York, From Actual Surveys by S.N. & D.G. Beers and Assistants. Philadelphia, Pa.: Stone and Stewart, 1866-1969 reprint.

The Northern Traveler; Containing the Routes to Niagara, Quebec, and the Springs with the Tour of New England. 2nd Edition. New York, N.Y.: A.T. Goodrich, 1826.

Perry, John, M.D. *An Analysis of Congress Spring, with Practical Remarks on Its Medical Properties* by John Steel, M.D. New York: Perry, 1861.

Prokopoff, Stephen and Siegfried, Joan. *The Nineteenth-Century Architecture of Saratoga Springs: Architecture Worth Saving in New York State.* New York, N.Y.: New York State Council on the Arts, 1970.

Puckhaber, Bernhard. *Saratogas.* Ballston Spa, N.Y.: Bernhard Puckhaber, 1976.

Saratoga and Waterford Directory, For 1877-1878. Saratoga Springs, N.Y.: J.H. Lant, 1877.

Saratoga, Ballston and Waterford Directory, For 1875-76. Saratoga Springs, N.Y.: J.H. Lant, 1875.

Saratoga Ilustrated: The Visitor's Guide to Saratoga Springs. New York, N.Y.: Taintor Bros., Merrill & Co., Publishers, 1876, 1882, 1886.

The Saratoga Sentinel. Saratoga Springs, N.Y.: Huling and Co., 1875-1885.

Saratoga Springs Directory, 1883-1884. Saratoga Springs, N.Y.: Kirwin and Williams, 1883.

Saratoga Springs Directory. Saratoga Springs, N.Y.: The Saratogian Company, 1894-1900.

"Saratoga Springs," *Harper's New Monthly Magazine.* New York, N.Y.: Harper's, 1876.

"Saratoga Springs: Historical, Industrial and Picturesque Saratoga", *Daily Saratogian,* supplement. Saratoga Springs, N.Y.: the Daily Saratogian, undated.

Saratoga Springs, Its Mineral Fountains, Drives, Hotels and Other Items of Interest: How to Enjoy a Visit. Saratoga Springs, N.Y.: Cozzens and Mingay, 1886.

Saratoga Springs: Souvenir, 50th Anniversary, The Saratogian, 1855-1905. Saratoga Springs, N.Y.: the Daily Saratogian, 1905.

Saratoga: Winter and Summer, An Epitome of the Early History, Romance, Legends and Characteristics of the Greatest of American Resorts. New York, N.Y.: Prentiss Ingraham, 1885.

The Saratogian Almanac. Saratoga Springs, N.Y.: Paul and Richie, 1878-1882. (titles vary)

The Saratogian Almanac. Saratoga Springs, N.Y.: The Saratogian, 1883-1896. (titles vary)

Sheppard, Nathan. *Saratoga Chips and Carlsbad Wafers.* New York, N.Y.: Funk & Wagnalls, Publishers, 1887.

Sorin, Gretchen Sullivan and Rehl, Jane. *Honorable Work: African Americans in the Resort Community of Saratoga Springs, 1870-1970.* Saratoga Springs, N.Y.: Historical Society of Saratoga Springs, 1992.

Souvenir of Floral Festival No.1 and Prospectus of a Greater Saratoga with Views and Plans of Proposed Park. Saratoga Springs, N.Y.: the Saratogian, September, 1894.

The Spouter. Ballston Spa, N.Y. and Concord, N.H.: Saratoga-Type Bottle Collectors Society, Vol. 1-51, 1982-97.

"The Springs at Saratoga". *New York Daily Graphic.* New York, N.Y.: New York Daily Graphic, August 19, 1878.

Stoddard, Seneca Ray. *Saratoga Springs,* 3rd Edition. Glens Falls, N.Y.: S.R. Stoddard, 1883.

Stone, William L. *Reminiscences of Saratoga and Ballston.* New York, N.Y.: R. Worthington, 1880.

Swanner, Grace Maguire. *Saratoga Queen of Spas.* Utica, N.Y.: North Country Books, 1988.

Sweeney, Beatrice. "Saratoga Springs." *Saratoga County Heritage,* pages 539-565. Ballston Spa, N.Y.: Saratoga County, 1974.

Sweeney, Beatrice. *The Grand Union Hotel: A Memorial and a Lament.* Saratoga Springs, N.Y.: Historical Society of Saratoga Springs, 1982.

Sylvester, Nathaniel Bartlett. *History of Saratoga County, New York.* Philadelphia, Pa.: Everts and Ensign, 1878.

Sylvester, Nathaniel Bartlett. *History of Saratoga County, New York,* prepared by Samuel T. Wiley and W. Scott Garner. New York, N.Y.: Gersham Publishing Co., 1893.

Taub, Marion and Beatrice Sweeney. *Bibliography of Research Materials on Saratoga Springs, New York.* Saratoga Springs, N.Y.: Saratoga Springs Public Library, 1977.

Waller, George. *Saratoga: Saga of an Impious Era.* Englewood Cliffs, N.J.: Prentice-Hall, 1966.

Unpublished Sources:

Divak, Yvonne. "The Orin Rugg Exhibit". November, 1985. Manuscript in Historical Society of Saratoga Springs, Saratoga Springs, N.Y.

Gilcoyne, Thomas. "Saratoga Racing Dates". Chart in National Museum of Racing and Hall of Fame, Saratoga Springs, N.Y.

Horne, Field. "Working Notes for Congress Park Tour". 1997. Manuscript in author's possession, Saratoga Springs, N.Y.

Rugg, Orin. "Letter from Harrison's Landing, Va". August 8, 1862. Historical Society of Saratoga Springs, Saratoga Springs, N.Y.

"Red Spring Register". Aug. 8, 1876-Aug 15, 1877. Journal in author's collection, Saratoga Springs, N. Y.

LIST OF PHOTOGRAPHS AND DATES

Chapter 8

INDEX